Theodorus Bailey Myers

The Tories: Loyalists in America

Being slight historical tracings: From the footprints of Sir John Johnson

Theodorus Bailey Myers

The Tories: Loyalists in America
Being slight historical tracings: From the footprints of Sir John Johnson

ISBN/EAN: 9783337233877

Printed in Europe, USA, Canada, Australia, Japan

Cover: Foto ©ninafisch / pixelio.de

More available books at **www.hansebooks.com**

The Tories or Loyalists

IN AMERICA

BEING

SLIGHT HISTORICAL TRACINGS, FROM THE
FOOTPRINTS OF SIR JOHN JOHNSON
AND HIS COTEMPORARIES IN
THE REVOLUTION.

BY

T. BAILEY MYERS.

"*Ab fas aut ab nefas.*"

Albany
Press of Joel Munsell's Sons
82 State Street
1882

THE TORIES OR LOYALISTS.

HE accompanying waifs, possessing in themselves as little intrinsic interest as continuity, are a few random footprints of Sir John Johnson's life of exile, spared by the tides of a century which have effaced many of his once deeper impressions on American affairs. They casually fell into the writer's historical collection, mingled with other imported manuscripts, proving at least, that some antiquarian in the old world had considered them worthy of preservation.

The knowledge that amongst such fragments have been found the key to valuable facts, and the elucidation of past events obscured by time, has, as we know, caused a growing interest in the preservation in public or private collections or in print, of anything of a public character, produced by the brain and hands of men who made some mark on their time before passing away.

What seems of little value to one, may become of interest to another, and we know that there are few things existing which have not a place when the problem of supply and demand is solved. Even a rock which has long cumbered the ground becomes valuable when broken up and concreted into a wall.

Although these papers referred to throw very little, and that a later light upon the unfortunate career of Sir John Johnson, which will be found more fully considered by experienced hands in the preceding pages, they have a value as a means of presenting incidentally, such letters of his cotemporaries as space permits, connected with events in which he participated. In themselves they contain little of historical interest and treat more of counting of the cost of war than of its more interesting details.

Some investigator of facts may find in them a suggestion, or possibly a warning, against the repetition of such unremunerative outlay, attending the more valuable loss of blood. To another, they may seem no more instructive, than the brick which the fool in the fable carried with him in his travels, as an illustration of the house in which he lived.

The knowledge that Mr. Stone, who has already supplemented his father's valuable service in furnishing interesting details of struggles between the colonists of France and England, and those of the Revolution on that debatable ground, the northern frontier, in which the romantic Valley of the Mohawk was often a base of British operations,[1] was occupied in connection with General de Peyster (an enthusiastic student and commentator on many of the military events of both continents), in preparing a brochure intended to illustrate the military career of Sir John Johnson, and aiming in a biographical sketch, to remove some of the unanswered obloquy which was piled upon him as the exiled adherent of a lost and unpopular cause,[2]

---

[1] The Life of Sir William Johnson and The Campaigns of General Burgoyne.

[2] As an illustration of the then widely prevailing sentiment, the citizens of Worcester, Mass., voted May 19, 1783, "That in the opinion of this town, it would be truly dangerous to the peace, happiness, liberty and safety of these States, to suffer those

with an Orderly Book as a basis, has induced the contribution of these fragments as an annex to their work.

These prefatory notes are added at Mr. Stone's suggestion.

The task of Gen. de Peyster would seem to any unbiased reader to be a natural one to a collateral descendant thus qualified, and infinitely more practicable since our own experiences in the great Civil War.

In the division of section, family and friends which it induced, in the bitterness of the feeling and vehement denunciation of motive and action it called forth, were reproduced those of the Revolution of 1776, only upon a grander scale. Then men weighed their duties and responsibilities, and the relative claims of the flag under which they were born, or those of the states in which they were located, and compared the grievances which had caused the separation from Great Britain with those claimed to have succeeded under that subsequent Union of the States. In recalling the terms of ridicule and reproach engendered by hatred, exchanged between the defenders of that Union and the Confederates, and the little credit given by either

who, the moment the bloody banners were displayed, abandoned their native land, turned parricides, and conspired to involve their country in tumult, ruin and blood, to become the subjects of and reside in this government; that it would be not only dangerous, but inconsistent with justice, policy, our past laws, the public faith, and the principles of a free and independent state, to admit them ourselves, or to have them forced upon us without our consent." * * * * "That until the further order of the government, they (the committees of Correspondence, Inspection and Safety), will, with decision, spirit, and firmness, endeavor to enforce and carry into execution the several laws of this Commonwealth, respecting these enemies of our rights, and the rights of mankind; give information, should they know of any obtruding themselves into any part of this State, suffer none to remain in this town, but cause to be confined immediately, for the purpose of transportation according to law, any that may presume to enter it." These were the general terms meted out to the Tories, recorded in the "Journal and Letters of Samuel Curwen, Judge of Admiralty," a "Harvard Man" of 1735, and in his time a valued citizen. Although not an active partisan he passed into exile through his scruples in 1775, but as an exceptional case was allowed to return, in the ensuing year, to live and die at his old home in Salem, in 1802.

to the sense of duty which actuated their opponents, we can understand, now that temporary feeling is rapidly passing away, that in the earlier struggle there clearly frequently existed as honest and as opposite convictions of right.

Surely the time has arrived when we can discuss without temper, the motives, and appreciate the loyalty to their government, the sacrifice of life and property, and the sufferings by confiscation and exile of that valuable material for continued citizenship — numbering at least twenty thousand of the inhabitants of a sparsely settled and devastated country — then transferred as Refugees into Nova Scotia and Canada[3] to form

---

[3] The following paper endorsed "160, Proposals for a General Naturalization Bill," from the contents and the appearance of the carefully written manuscript, and of the observations which follow it, was evidently submitted to Parliament soon after the Peace — it is considered worthy of a place, as showing the value attached by the British Government to her exiled adherents, and her desire to retain them in her remaining Colonies, as to her a tried element of population. It will be observed that while providing for all classes of Tories, it ingeniously invites the "Rebels," whom it assumes to be already dissatisfied with their new experiment, to join them.

"THE INHABITANTS OF THE UNITED STATES who took part with the British Government by remaining or by continuing within the Lines during the War in America, and who have since removed into any part of the British Dominions having never done anything to forfeit their original rights and privileges as British Subjects, are in that respect, in the same situation as at first, and have no want of any act of Parliament on that account. Some of the Americans who did not remove within the Lines, have continued obstinately Non-jurors to the United States to this day. These men during the War suffered much in their property by the payment of double Taxes, and underwent many personal inconveniences, and even insults, and though their situation may be rendered somewhat more Tolerable by the Peace, yet it must be sufficiently disagreeable to induce them to change it, and to remove within the British Dominions, as soon as they conveniently can do it. In what light are they to be regarded, on their arrival in Nova Scotia, or Canada, or elsewhere in the British Dominion? Are they still British Subjects, or must they be at the expense of soliciting Acts of Naturalization? They were originally Natural Born Subjects, they took the Oath of Allegiance to the Crown of Great Britain, and they have never taken any other Oath of Allegiance, how then can they consistently with common reason and equity be regarded as Aliens, and on their arrival in the British Dominions, to claim privileges which are their birthright, and which they have never forfeited by any Act of Theirs, be put to the expense of being naturalized? Are they not rather to be treated as subjects returning from a foreign country, in which adverse Circumstances have detained them, contrary to their Inclinations and

the best elements of population in a country in which they declared on their sad departure, they expected to endure " nine months of winter and three of cold weather in each year."

When the subsequent war of 1812 was carried to, and across the Canadian frontier, our soldiers found in this rejected material their most determined opponents. They naturally had little in common with those, once their countrymen, but then only geographically their neighbors, still politically their foes, and the

Wishes? There are in the United States, men of a different description, who collectively form a numerous Body, men who from the first uniformly refused to take any active part against the British Government, who for some time refused to take the Oath of Allegiance to the United States, but were by the force of Vexations, personal insult, and menaces, finally brought to submit to preserve their estates from confiscation, and themselves and families from suffering the last extremities of Want and Misery. Those men, from their coming in so late, and by compulsion, to acknowledge the Supremacy of the United States, *did not regain either the Friendship or Confidence of their Countrymen*, they simply brought their persons and property within the protection of the Law, and even that was in some instances at least, but nominally such. These men, whose political principles have not been changed, wish to remove, if it could be done on any Valuable Terms. But they must think it a hard case to be considered as Aliens, and be obliged to sue for Acts of Naturalization, at a great and ruinous expense and Loss of Time, and to pray and pay dearly to be declared, what they are conscious in their Hearts, that they have ever been, British Subjects. The last and most numerous Class, and who have neither Law or Equity to urge, but good policy only, are Merchants, the middle and lower Orders of Farmers, Shipwrights, Fishermen and Sailors. That is, those of them who voluntarily, and without any Force or compulsion, took an early and active part in favor of the Revolution, who at the Time judging from appearances and representations made to them, of Absolute Subjection and Slavery on the one hand, and the prospect of Liberty, an exemption from Taxes, and unbounded and unrestrained Commerce on the other, were naturally led, and as it were necessarily impelled, by the Motives and Objects before them, to take the part which they then took, but who on reflection and experience perceive their Error, find all those favorable prospects vanished, and in their place Factions and Licentiousness predominant, their persons or Estates loaded with intolerable Taxes, and their Commerce, more circumscribed and burthened than ever, they are solicitous to regain their former political situation, by removing within the British Dominions, and returning to their Ancient and hereditary Allegiance, if they can be received and admitted to the same privileges, as others of their rank and orders in Life, are entitled to. With regard to the first, that is, the Lovalists already removed, there can be no question. For the two next, the actual non-jurors who are as such to this day, and those who by Violence and Menaces, were forced to take Oaths of Allegiance to the New Government, much may be urged in their favor, both in Law and Equity. As to the re-admission of the latter, by much the most numerous Body, and rapidly increasing, political considerations and motives alone can be urged, and those if all the circum-

occupants of their forfeited homes. Compare this adjustment in 1783 with the more wise policy of our government in the late struggle, where, after the suppression of armed resistance, the citizens were soon restored to civil rights, and their property — not lost by military results, and the attendant reduction of values — and were reunited in a common administration of public affairs.

History written in the progress or at the termination of a war, is usually formed like the government by the victorious

stances are understood, and the consequences fully examined into, will prove as forcible as anything that can be urged for the former. It is therefore proposed that a General Declaratory Act should be passed, putting the situation of all those who have already removed from the United States, and Settled in any part of the British Dominions, beyond any future question or doubt, declaring that all who were formerly British Subjects in any part of the United States or born of Parents who were British Subjects in those States, previous to the late Treaty of Peace, shall on their removal into any part of the British Dominions in America, either on the Continent, or in the West India Islands, and on taking and subscribing the Oath and declaration which shall be acquired by them, shall be admitted to all the rights and privileges of free and natural born subjects of Great Britain, provided that their removal, and taking the Oath be within four years from the passing such Act, provided also that they bring certificates of their having been formerly British Subjects, in the United States when Colonies, or the Children of such Subjects. The oaths to be administered by Magistrates named for that purpose, and recorded in the public Records of the province or Colony where the same shall be taken.

1st Observation. There will be no objection to that part of such an Act, as refers to the Declared, and actually removed Loyalist.

2d Observation. In regard to the two second, no material exception can be taken to persons continuing. Non-jurors are Loyalists, not yet removed within the British Dominion, their *not removing on the evacuation of New York is no Objection, as too many were then under an absolute and pressing necessity to remove, so that their remaining, became a favor to those who did remove, and those forced to submit to the Oath imposed upon them, are to be considered as being nearly in the same predicament.*

But 3dly, if these are admitted, it is hardly possible to prevent the last description from coming in under their Character, not inconsistent with that of a Merchant, a Farmer, a Shipwright, a Fisherman, or a Sailor, *these orders of men are immediately wanted, and in Great Numbers, in Nova Scotia and Canada, and as those orders of men find themselves pressed by taxes in the United States and their Commerce restricted as Aliens and Foreigners by this and other Nations, and burthened with duties and imports by their own Government they will naturally incline to remove and such an encouragement may probably render Nova Scotia and Canada populous, and rich in a very few years.*

sentiment. *Vae victis!* It is left to posterity in most cases to do justice to the unfortunate.

In Painting and Cartography, truth to nature, and accuracy, are indispensible to value. We continue our appreciation of Old Masters, and admire and even yet sail by the carefully based and grandly executed Charts of the earlier centuries; while we also accept the new school of Art, as well as the improved Maps which several nations, notably including our own vie in perfecting.[4] Why should not History, which records, the action of what is held as nature's noblest work, be ranked as a kindred art? While it would be the act of a vandal to alter an old masterpiece, it may be the duty of an humble painter to restore it, and the right of all Artists to seek to improve upon it.

No careful cross reader has failed to detect palpable errors in history, possibly injected in hasty compilation, from ill founded rumor, misconception, or partisan zeal, perhaps allowed to remain until too late for available cotemporaneous correction, by the indifference, or individuality, of even a worthy actor. It would seem as though in all ages, men, while naturally desiring to be recorded as famous in public affairs, or in the field, have permitted the notable achievements of their assistants to be condensed in their own. Often the resort to Official Records has corrected hasty narrative and changed

---

[4] An examination of the progress of this science in essential details, although artistic embellishment is less used than formerly, would appear interesting to every one connected with some portion of the surface delineated.

The American " Geographical Society," only a few years since still a problematical undertaking, now grown into a widely appreciated and amply sustained fact; has largely through the unremitting attention of its President, Chief Justice Daly, collected in its Map-room one of the most complete series ever formed by a technical institution, affording an opportunity to those who would appreciate Cartography to examine its claim to be recognized as high Art.

the complexion of what has long been accepted as facts. Such investigations even centuries after, when applied to the history of our late war, or that we are now making, will doubtless prove the shears of Nemesis and continue to clip off a surplus fringe of long seated error.

To aid in such researches and to make its illustration more complete, Old letters, Documents and Diaries [5] of public interest have each a use. Letters we oftenest rely upon for cotemporary testimony. Diaries kept for personal reference or amusement, even when meagre in detail, but written without the intention of publication, or of influencing the views of others, and so possessing the value of disinterested testimony at the period as to events, persons and dates, have furnished valuable acquisitions to printed history for the reason that they were records of personal impression only and reserved until excitement had passed away. The Orderly Books or Diaries of regiments, have also afforded interesting details of service, against accepted error or conflicting testimony, fixing dates, positions, the number and description of a force, and the compass of its movements, and when annotated by a skillful hand

[5] The "History of New York, in the Revolutionary War," by the able but cynical Judge Thomas Jones — published through the liberality of one of his relatives, Mr. John D. Jones, and ably edited by another, Mr. Edward Floyd de Lancey, under the auspices of the New York Historical Society in 1879, with copious notes and references, is a rich mine to which any person interested in this subject, may profitably turn from this merely suggestive commentary. The fierce impartiality with which he criticises Whig and Tory, soldier and civilian, induces additional credence to the many curious facts he recorded in exile, of men and events with which he was familiar. A letter from General Huntington to his son, while occupying his fine town house, east of the City Hall, — in that collection—expresses gratitude to him for planting the fruit he was enjoying at his quarters, and its fine view of the harbor. His country estate at Fort Neck, is preserved in the family by an entail that prevented confiscation. This, even with the letter books of Governor Cadwallader Colden, published by that Society, cross read with Judge William Smith's "History of the Province of New York," would in themselves afford an opening for a research similar to that of Carlyle, for the truthful inwardness of affairs at that period, in the city.

and published, have furnished the clew to much information otherwise lost from the woof of history.

Those who have found entertainment in delving into the controversial folios of partisan writers, full of what appeared to them to be truths, have realized how easily, and honestly, men may differ.

In England in the varied changes in the control of a divided people, by Charles I, or by the Parliament, the Commonwealth or the Restoration, those of each in turn had the opportunity of disseminating such convictions, to approving readers, and for posterity to consider and compare. As an example of their utility, it was amongst such discordant narrations—much of which he styled "Shot Rubbish"—that Carlyle, and others, have searched analogically for facts, and it was from such neglected authorities that he derived many of the conclusions, which give color to his illustration of the "Letters and Speeches of Oliver Cromwell," probably destined to survive those crude "Reminiscences" of his own career, which have recently disappointed his appreciators. The peculiarities of his inverted expression, and thought provoking style, once comprehended, the result of those researches appears to present to the reader, even in a concentrated form, the man, his impulses, and surroundings, often overlooked before in the consideration of the narrative of his remarkable career.

From the mass of such conflicting testimony, has also been in part exhumed at different periods, the material from which such accepted writers as Hume, Smollett, Gibbon, Robertson, Macauley, Alison, Mahon, and many others less broadly known, have erected with the increasing impartiality attending later investigation, Monuments to their country, creditable to the workmen. Each, in his way has apparently sought to form safe resting places for conviction, by substituting what, after careful inspection, appeared to possess the solidity of fact, for what the impulse of the hour had concreted, but time, and closer investigation, pronounced unreliable.

Some of such investigators, have been impressed with certain coincidences between that Great English Revolution, and our own of 1776.

Arising, in each case amongst the same race, firm in conviction and resolute in assertion, inspired by similar complaints of oppression and sense of right, resulting alike in divided sentiment as to the proper extent of Prerogative, and the remedy against its encroachments, involving at first, heated discussion in public assemblies, filling the minds of many well meaning citizens with doubt as to a course rendered difficult to fix upon by conflicting ties or interests, and finally precipitating in one case the Mother Country and in the other her Colonies, into the horrors of Civil War, seeming in many particulars to be but the renewal of a suspended conflict.

By the result of both of these domestic struggles many who had in former peaceful times been held as valuable citizens, were impoverished and driven into exile [6] — in the former from the

---

[6] The following is a letter from John Cruger, Esq., Mayor of New York from 1739 to 1744, and from 1757 to 1766, and Speaker of the Assembly of 1775. He was then a prisoner on parole at the residence of his brother-in-law Peter Van Schaack, the celebrated lawyer, whose wife soon after died from want of proper medical treatment in New York, access to which the regulations of war precluded.

KINDERHOOK, *April* 12, 1778.

SIR :

I have Rec'd your favor & am Extremely Sorry that any Impediment has arisen in the Way of my going to New York. When I Recd Genl Gates' permission Upon Condition of my Engaging to fulfil the Exchange he proposed, I wrote him I did not chuse to go Upon a condition which it might be out of my

varied successes, drawn from both of the contending factions—
affording opportunity to each in turn, to develope the smaller
characteristics of nature, in the uses of success as an opportunity
for the harsh assertion of authority, in resorting to confiscation,
exile and individual suffering, in the changes of property as well
as of place.

Now, if we can judge from history and observation, both
Cavalier and Roundhead are looked back upon by their descendants and their successors with equal respect, and their actions
as the result of conviction, with a common pride. The
impressions of the past have been more readily forgotten, in the
activity of the present by a large portion of a people, attached
like our own to a government which has developed, in the experience of past strife the elasticity of its institutions, and of a
progressive energy in rebounding after a strain, to even a
stronger tension.

One element of its population, many of the people of
Ireland, from circumstances yet adhere to their old prejudices, and still recall Cromwell's severity in his invasion, and

power to perform. Upon which he wrote me as your Excellency Will Recollect
from his Letter, that he looked to Sir Henry Clinton for the performance of Any
Engagement I should make, and I have reason to think from What I then and have
since heard that this matter was settled between these two Generals. Could I have
foreseen that it was Possible that this wd have been prevented taking place, I Should
I am sure have had no difficulty in Getting the Genls passport Upon which several
have gone down, Even after he quitted Albany, Altho I cannot it Seems be so
fortunate. Perhaps upon Considering this matter, Your Excellency will be of
opinion that Sir Henry Clinton will perform what Genl Gates Relied Upon him for,
however diffident your Excellency may be of Genl Jones Who is I believe an Inferior
Officer to Sir Henry Clinton. Especially as I shall then go down Upon the Confidence between him and Genl Gates & not upon any promise of Genl Jones. If
your Excellency still entertain doubts, I will be content to go down with one Servant
only (Leaving my family and Effects,) upon Parole to return if an Exchange cannot
be Effected. I sincerely Request of Your Excellency, so far as you consistently can, to
take my situation into Consideration, and I hope when you Reflect on ye age and
Infirmity of my sister and Self, & the great Inconveniency which we Labour Under
here, You Will Readily fall upon some Means to Extricate Us Out of our Difficultys

King William's success at the Battle of the Boyne, with equal bitterness. They had never cheerfully transferred their adhesion from the house of Stewart to either the Prince of Orange or that of Hanover. Many of them, including those of the best element had been driven by that war and its results, into France and other countries, often to become from choice soldiers, in many cases still represented by their descendants, with the same courage which turned the current of the fight at Fontenoy, and made the command of the regiment Dillon, long hereditary. Others came to America, replacing the departed loyalists, soon exceeding them in numbers, and rapidly increasing as we know, until in many sections they form a very large element of population. Their hereditary prejudices and their natural tendency to politics, perhaps inspired by the consideration of their grievances, the apparent error of the government in not fostering their manufacturies, industries and universal education, have perhaps united to produce for generations political agitations and

Which I shall be happy to Retaliate by Every means in my power, to procure the Enlargement of any family, which may be desirous of moving out of New York.
I have the honour to be With great Esteem
Yr Ex. Most Obed &
Very humb. Servt

His Ex. Gov. Clinton.
JOHN CRUGER.

GOVERNOR CLINTON's ANSWER.

POUGHKEEPSIE, *April* 19, 1778.

SIR:

I have received your letter of the 12th Instant & in Answer thereto, am reduced to the necessity of Informing you that I cannot consent to your going to New York in any other way than that of exchange. The conduct of Messrs. Wallace, Sherbrooke & several others who were indulged to go in on Parole & to return, or send out some citizens, in exchange, has rendered the like indulgence to others altogether improper. At any rate the intercourse between the Country & City will be totally prohibited for some Weeks to come as the Commanding Officer, were I ever so willing, will not suffer any Persons to pass the Posts below. I shall be always ready Sir to grant you every Indulgence consistent with the Duty of my Office.
I am Sir Your Most Obedt. Servt,

John Cruger, Esq.
(GEORGE CLINTON.)

misunderstandings at home, and probably induced an immense emigration, who by becoming citizens, necessarily separate themselves politically from their country and have in the seaboard cities especially, largely acquired that control of which they were deprived in their old home, centuries ago.

It is a singular paradox, attending the gigantic prosperity of the country, that while one large class of citizens neglect, in the excitement of business occupations, even the ordinary duty of electors, another often abandon the opportunities for solid prosperity and wealth, attracted by the glitter of authority and perhaps ephemeral salary, and in seeking office devote their lives to "politics," and their advancement to the control of its dispensers.

While the majority of the people of Great Britain accepted the House of Hanover cheerfully, if coldly, they took no interest in the complications of the first two sovereigns, in protecting their birthplace and Principality on the continent. Its position involved them in the "Seven Years' War"—without eventual advantage, and imposed upon them a heavy indebtedness, partially to meet which, in the reign of George III, the attempted taxation of his American colonies, also its seat, was resorted to, which afforded them their opportunity.

The history prepared by a conquered enemy is generally little accepted by the victor, beyond its use in illustrating some strategic detail. Its statements of any motives, or of rights invaded, or injustice done, would be as indifferently received as he argument of a case after the jury had retired — a barren effort which is believed to have at times affected intellects. That of the English writers, as to the Revolutionary war has rarely been generally accepted or studied, in search for even minor particulars, by those satisfied with results. In our own histories, while doing justice to the general details of the origin and progress of the conflict, little attention was naturally given to personal conviction, or to apparent necessity, as influencing the action of any ally of the enemy, while resisting the success of a struggle for Independence. Tory and Hessian, have been rated with the Indian, and all considered the worst elements of a bad cause, best remembered as the perpetrators of those ravages of war, impressed more strongly, by tradition and early history, upon the communities where they occur, than any nobler action, and therefore more likely to survive. That they soon departed, leaving neither apologist nor vindicator, seems to afford a sufficient reason for some just consideration of their then position, a century later.

We have realized some "modern instances" since, where prejudice has unduly obscured, or partiality unreasonably brightened, the records of the wrestlers in a world of action.

The annexation of Texas — a Republic then recently carved out of the territory of a friendly power, while it slumbered—may be recalled by some as having presented a question of such then apparently vast importance, as to have seemed for a time to shake the foundation of our own government. Strict constructionists of law, and those watchful of the integrity of our avowed national policy, entered into vehement protest against an act for which they could discover no authority, and its inevitable result, in a war with a weaker power, to acquire by force a territory, then looked upon without coveting it, by a large portion of the people. The debates in Congress on the subject, will survive as long as the government they affected by their results, as characterized by marked ability and vehemence, for there were surely *many* statesmen in Congress at that period. When the war was precipitated, all differences were speedily buried and the

Maxim "Our Country Right or Wrong," silenced dissent or opposition and carried brave men of both factions in concert to the field.[7] Many Americans residing in Mexican Territory, under such protection as it could afford to their property, naturally placed themselves under their national colors. We can conceive that if the Mexican forces had then been able to invade the United States, the action of *her* citizens residing within their borders and enjoying their protection would have been a subject for jealous scrutiny! Their duty to the flag under which they were born, unless abandoned by a new allegiance, could not be questioned, while its exercise against the government that had protected them would have been considered as an act of aggravated hostility.

In our Civil War the manhood of the country of an available age largely buried political dissensions, and when the question was narrowed to that of the supremacy of the flag, hastened to the front. When such voluntary material for its maintenance seemed exhausted, the additional inducement of large bounties was added to the customary pay to stimulate patriotism, or compensate for the time diverted from personal enterprise. It was then noticed that the representation of

[7] The anxiety to obtain service in this war, and the enthusiasm which attended its progress, when once precipitated must be recalled by many. More troops were offered than could be used, and the Southern and Southwestern States, more sectionally interested in the acquisition of new territory, continually pressed the offer of additional regiments. Those of New York, which succeeded in obtaining orders, did good service in Mexico and California, while others offered could find no place. The contributor recalls how, although opposed to the annexation from surrounding association, and scarcely qualified by age as an elector, happening to be, for the second time, aid de camp to a notable Governor of the old school, and thus a Colonel on the Peace Establishment, inspired by the sentiment of the moment, he committed that operation so painful to all soldiers, actual or implied, waived his rank and raised a company, in a regiment which was so denied the privilege of fame or the possibility of failure. The effort was an effect of the electricity with which all were charged, impressing even a titular soldier with the value of his sword, rather than of his rank.

other nationalities in our ranks was largely increased. In the rising of a government in its force to preserve its existence, the way was necessarily subordinated to the means, and all were acceptable. Even the Chinese, valueless as an elector, would have been welcome in the hour of danger, to fight for a nationality open to all others, as the home of liberty. It was noticeable also, that when hostilities finally ensued, many who had long excited by their persistent eloquence the people of both sections to seek for, to cherish, if not to magnify differences, until a perhaps inevitable conflict was precipitated, did not crowd into the ranks, or if in Congress, all follow the example of that gallant Senator, Edward D. Baker, a proto-martyr of that body in the conflict, who falling at the head of his regiment at Balls Bluff, while practically advancing his plea for the Union, made a more lasting impression than words addressed to applauding galleries, by men of either section fired by zeal, who failed to afterwards emphasize the depth of their convictions, by service in the field.

Those who did this followed an old precedent, established by members of both houses of Parliament in the English Civil War, where, as an example, Lucius Cary, Viscount Falkland[a],

---

[a] Clarendon in his "History of the Great Rebellion" thus records the virtues of one who might have been an agreeable and instructive associate, "he was a person of such prodigious parts of learning and knowledge, and of that inimitable sweetness and delight in conversation, and of so flowing and obliging a humanity and goodness to mankind, and of that primitive simplicity and integrity of life, that if there were no other brand upon the odious and accursed Civil War than that single loss, it must be most infamous to all posterity." He was deeply depressed by the compass which he foresaw in the conflict, frequently cried to himself "Peace, Peace," and doubting its speedy coming; having accompanied the King at Edgehill, Oxford and Gloucester, being his Secretary of State, he threw himself as a volunteer into the front rank of Lord Byron's regiment, at the battle of Newberry, and was killed by a musket ball.

"Thus Falkland died the generous and the just," at least another martyr to honest convictions.

a conscientious patriot, and one of the first to rise in Parliament in opposition to grievances, was also one of the earliest to voluntarily die in defence of his sovereign, when he considered that the claims for redress were pressed too far. Many members of our Continental Congress also displayed by their service in the field, their conviction that a statesman whether involuntary, hereditary or professional, does not lessen his official dignity, by contact in the ranks even with those who had not sympathized in the *discussion*, until forced into the *conflict* by results.

Gallant service in both the council and the field would appear to be unanswerable evidences of at least honest convictions.[9]

The Trumpeter, in another fable, would appear to have been properly denied immunity, as a non-combatant, for the reason that he incited bloodshed by his noisy brass. It had already

> [9] An example of this disinterested appreciation of a double duty, may be cited in Lewis Morris, a Signer of the Declaration of Independence, a member of Congress, grandson of a Colonial Governor of New Jersey, in his turn the son of an English officer of Cromwell's army, who had made America his refuge at the Restoration— the proprietor of a Manor of some thousands of acres called Morrisania, in Westchester, New York, and an honored citizen, who, although like the Johnsons', with much to lose personally, for the prospect of a gain by a change of government, threw his fortunes into an opposite scale. His love to freedom, probably hereditary, early carried him into public life, and with his beautiful home desolated, his family scattered, his thousand of acres of woodland felled and the British ships lying within cannon shot of his mansion, he was, at the time this letter was written, sitting in Congress and commanding a disaffected Brigade, in the southern part of Westchester County, the most disloyal portion of a Tory State. It is taken from the original:
>
> PHILADELPHIA, *September* 24, 1776.
>
> SIR:
>
> I had the honor to receive your Letter accompanying the Resolve of Congress relative to my return to resume the command of my Brigade, at a time when the State to which I belong is invaded, and particularly as I am honored with a military command, I esteem it my duty to account for my absence. Since my arrival at Philadelphia, the State of New York has had no more than a representative in Congress, and as the Gentlemen of the Committee of Indian Affairs were mostly out of Town, the whole of that necessary business has been devolved upon me. *My family have been obliged to desert their home, and meeting with them in this place,*

been discovered, that it was easier to excite than to allay a conflict, and that only the peacemaker *was* blessed.

There is a middle course, which caution has often suggested to personal interest, in the consideration of all untried enterprises; that of uniting with neither party, while coquetting with, and appearing to entertain, the views of both. From any imputation of such littleness, at least, Johnson and his Tory associates would appear to have been free, as the evidence of their offence was in their undisguised coöperation.

When the French fleet, with Rochambeau's army, was groping its way in search of Newport and towards Yorktown, on the 10th of July, 1780, through Martha's Vineyard, and the fogs which yatchsmen so often deplore, an islander boarded the Conquerant, 74 — conveying Generals the Baron de Vioménel, Count de Custine, who soon after led the advanced troops to

altogether unprovided, I have been under the necessity of delaying the time of my stay until I could fix them in some situation where they could be accommodated. This distress of my Family on this occasion made it my particular duty to attend to them, and which I flatter myself will be justifiable upon every principle of justice. The situation of my Brigade I was convinced was well known to the Convention, I apprehended that not more than a Colonel's command was left in it, and as such did not think my presence was so absolutely necessary. I have thought that the existence of such a Brigade, in which were so many disaffected persons, was dangerous to the cause as well as to my own life. But being desirous to participate in the virtuous opposition to the British Tyrant, I had determined as soon as possible to join Gen. Washington and contribute my assistance to him, prompted in the first instance by a Love of my Country, and in the next place the preservation of my property, being thoroughly convinced that unless we conquer I am ruined. However in obedience to the command of Convention I shall prepare with all possible. expedition to set out for Westchester, and will endeavor to execute any orders they may be pleased to give to the utmost of my ability.

I have the honor to subscribe myself, Sir, Your obliged and Obed't Humble Servant, LEWIS MORRIS.
(To the President of the Provincial Congress of New York).

He afterwards returned to service, was a Major General and had, as his fellow officers, three of his sons. Of his own brothers, Staats Long continued in the British service, became a Lieutenant General. Richard was a Judge of Admiralty, and Gouverneur the well esteemed Diplomatist and Congressman.

the Peninsula and performed valuable service there, and many officers and men of those auxilliaries —and who was useful as a pilot bringing valuable information, as to the Americans still holding Rhode Island,[10] "he was a good man"—says the Chief Commissary who was daily bottling up facts for our later refreshment—" and *displayed intelligence. He was neither a Royalist, or Insurgent, but a friend of everybody, as he told us with much simplicity.*" As the arrival of this expected assistance was an *occasion* for the expression of pleasure, and as the struggle it was coming to aid in terminating had long given opportunity for the formation of an opinion, it seems clear that he was a Loyalist, and yet in a condition to avail himself of the rapidly approaching success, with all the privileges of a patriot.

But courage based upon even *erroneous conviction* may claim respect. A generous opponent after success in defeating an object which from principle he has opposed, is often the earliest reconciled, and a heart conscious of the duty of loyalty, most open to forgive an honest but mistaken conception.

Thus, in later years, after time for comparison of events and reflection, such appreciation has even extended over the seas to the adherents of the Pretender, who lost their lives and estates in a hopeless effort to restore the unfortunate house of Stuart, to whom their fathers owed allegiance ; when realizing how that history has also in a way repeated itself in our own land, largely colonized by the exiles of both parties in England's civil wars, and how a similar sentiment inspired many good men, mis-

[10] Journal of Claude Blanchard, edited by Wm. Duane and Thos. Balch, Albany, 1876.
During the season of 1881, they were said by the Port officials to be more continuous than for sixteen years, and the whole eastern and the north-eastern coast resounded with the music of the fog horn, with little visible to the cruisers' eye.

takenly as the result proved, to endeavor to sustain the existing government; and some incidentally to follow or imitate such a leader as Sir John Johnson, in his effort to reclaim his inheritance by the same force that had been used in his eviction. His Scotch, Irish and German tenantry and his Indian allies, whose memory has come down to us as terrible as that of the " Black Douglas " with which babies of the Border were once hushed to sleep, were the same appliances long turned by his predecessor with general approval against the French. The barbarities attending his expedition, if greater than those recorded in all that partisan warfare, may, at this distance of time, be attributed to the bitter sentiment of divided neighborhood and broken friendship, the retaliation of the exile against him who retained or had acquired his home.

In our recent struggle we learned again that many foreign soldiers voluntarily came as has been stated, and accepted service on either side, for glory or for pay, indifferent to the cause; and also that old neighbors were often the fiercest opponents when meeting in strife.

If, in the light of that experience, there was one whose adhesion to the British Government in 1776 appears most readily accounted for, it would seem to be that of Sir John Johnson. His position as an officer in his King's service made it natural to a soldier; the personal honor of knighthood from the King's hand while in London, must have influenced his sympathy, aside from the hereditary sense of gratitude for the great bounties and trust conferred on his father.

That father dying in 1774 escaped the responsibility which fell upon his son. It is unnecessary to fully recall the career of Sir William Johnson who was probably the most remarkable, if not the most distinguished, character in American colonial history.

His coming as a youth from Ireland into the then wild Mohawk valley as the agent of his uncle, Admiral Sir Peter Warren, whose " great and veteran service " to this State, was rewarded in part with the means to secure an estate of 15,000 acres named " Warren's Bush " and afterwards by the gift from the city of New York of a suburban estate—called Chelsea, and now embedded in its limits—especially for his service in the capture of Louisburg ;" his succession from a pioneer planter and country store keeper to the control of the Six Nations of Indians, once the most powerful race on the Northern American Continent, who were likened to the Romans from the extent of their invasions from their northern home, west to the Falls of the Ohio, and south to the waters of Carolina.

" The capture of Louisburg, the key to Canada, skillfully fortified by a pupil of Vauban, garrisoned by regular French troops, and also protected by vessels of war, by 6,000 Provincials, commanded by " Mr. Pepperel a trader of Piscataqua," as colonel of the largest regiment, was a subject of world-wide wonder at the time, and may still be considered as one of the great military achievements on this continent. Its conception was due to the indefatigable Governor Shirley.

THE FOLLOWING COMMISSION given by Governor Shirley, when commanding *all* the Forces in North America, and signed by Lord Stirling, then Mr. Alexander, a young gentleman of fortune, when acquiring as an amateur the military knowledge which he supplemented by his gallantry, at the Battle of Long Island and in other service, shows the formality with which Indians were regularly commissioned, and educated in the warfare then waging against the French, subsequently turned against the Colonists whom they were then protecting. While the *use* of the Indians was complained of by civilized opponents in both cases, their employment had become habitual.

BY HIS EXCELLENCY, MAJOR GENERAL SHIRLEY, COMMANDER-IN CHIEF OF ALL HIS MAJESTY'S FORCES IN NORTH AMERICA,

To Tawenoe, Greeting :

By Virtue of the Power and Authority to me Granted by His Majesty and reposing especial Trust and Confidence in your *Faithfulness, Attachment and Loyalty* to His most sacred Majesty, King George the Second. I do appoint you, the said Tawenoe,

They might then become the balance of power between the English and French colonies, and are now, from the loss of such civilizing authority mainly extinct, enjoying in happier hunting grounds, freedom from the inevitable progress of the white man, before which they steadily pass away, making room for advancing cultivation.

Soon, his acquisition of military and civil power, of influence and estate, until he had become a viceroy in authority, with a princely personal domain, showed a rapid appreciation of his new surroundings. His intimate knowledge of the character of the Indians, his justice and wisdom in their control, their devotion to him, and his adaptation to their customs and language; his defence of the French border and his expeditions into their dominions, until dying a Baronet, a Major General, and Superintendent of Indian affairs, are matters that should be familiar to every reader.

His home, "Johnson Hall," was the theatre of much romantic incident connected with colonial history, and visited at intervals by most of the distinguished men on the

---

to be *Lieutenant of Indians* employed in the present Expedition for removing the French Encroachments at Niagara, and elsewhere on Lake Ontario, and you are faithfully to discharge the Duty of a Lieutenant of the Indians aforesaid.

GIVEN under my Hand and Seal at Arms, at the Camp at Oswego, on Lake Ontario, the first day of September, 1755. W. SHIRLEY.
By His Excellency's Command,
WM. ALEXANDER, Sec'y.[7]

Sir William Pepperel died a baronet, and his successor living to be deprived, his estate also passed into exile. It may be proper to mention, as one of the historical doubts which confuse the reader, that Dr. Dwight has claimed for General Lyman, the second in command, the principal credit for the defeat of Baron Dieskau near Lake George, by Sir William Johnson (Appendix) with the New England, New York and New Jersey Provincials, which aided to relieve the alarm created by Gen. Braddock's disaster, with another division of the army. There was great jealousy at this time between the New England and New York Provincial Troops. It was on such evidences of their skill in arms, that the self reliance of the Colonists in the coming struggle was founded.

continent. Their letters addressed to him on various affairs of state, with replies showing condensation of varied intelligence, conveyed in the graceful penmanship of a ready writer, are still preserved—some in the collection referred to—attesting a life of labor in the public service.

In this however, he found opportunity to attend to many personal duties, incident to his position and capacity. Isolated, and only restricted by the orders of the Government, which from better local appreciation of necessities, he alone, as its agent, had ventured to disregard; with an increasing neighborhood of many nationalities, English, Scotch, Irish, German and Hollander, as compatriots or tenantry, appealing to him for counsel in every relation of life, from the cradle to the grave, he advised and protected the living, and was burthened with trusts by the dead,[12] cheerfully fulfilling his duties to the lowly as a bountiful benefactor, and hospitably entertaining them with the great, who resorted to the hall, when amusing their leisure time with hardy sports and athletic games. He appears to have afforded an example to those charged with the control of the destinies of aggregates of men.

[12] The accompanying document appears worthy of reproduction, as a pen sketch affording a glimpse of this early backwoods life. As rough in autographic execution as its surroundings, it chances to place on one paper the names, and to show the meeting, of some historical celebrities of border life, friends soon to be divided in strife. The two Johnsons, General Nicholas "Herckmer," as he boldly but roughly writes himself,—in the year in which he was erecting the spacious brick mansion called his "Castle", which survives him near Little Falls,— destined afterwards to sit on the saddle of his dead horse, reclining against a tree, smoking his pipe, and issuing his orders, when mortally wounded in the battle of Oriskany, by the Tories and Indians of St. Leger and Sir John. Colonel Peter Schuyler, for a time acting as Colonial Governor of New York, called "Quider." by the Mohawks, whom he had led successfully against the French, and whom they trusted and loved, and Abraham Yates, Jun., subsequently an early Senator, both of the last at times Mayors of the important border city of Albany. With these are others, not unknown in that local history, although making as feeble impression on their times as on the paper, yet as necessary as are the minor connecting links in Genealogy.

He devoted much attention also, to the erection of churches and schools—even selecting with his intimate knowledge of the Mohawk dialect, the hymns to be sung—and to the education [13] and spiritual welfare of his savage neighbors, in his relations with whom there was much to recall the habits of the Patriarchs, and to account for this special interest in their progress which was probably remembered in the fidelity of four of the tribes, the Onondagas, Cayugas, Senecas and Mohawks, to his son, while the Oneidas alone supported the Americans, after vigorous efforts had been made to secure them all.

One of the latest objects of his attention was the publication of a new edition of the " Book of Common Prayer," to supply the place of the " Mohawk Prayer Book " printed in 1715, on

---

[13] From Rev. Eleazer Wheeluck, founder and President of Dartmouth College, and celebrated for his success and usefulness in his extended labors to educate and civilize the Indians. Amongst his pupils was Joseph Brant.

DARTMOUTH COLLEGE, IN NEW HAMPSHIRE, *Feb.* 27, 1773,

HON. SIR :

The bearers, Basteen and Lewis, Indians of the Tribe of Lorett, have been several months at my school, and have from the first appeared to have an uncommon thirst for Learning, have been diligent at their studies and have made good Proficiency for the Time therein. They appear to be rational, manly, spirited, courteous, graceful and obliging far beyond what I have found common to Indians, and I have observed no undue appetite in them for Strong Drink. They have often expressed a desire to see your Honor since they have lived with me, and now at their Desire I have consented to their making you this Visit.

I esteem them the most promising young Indians I have ever seen, and the most likely to answer the great and good ends of an Education, and I hope their going among their brethren in your parts will have no bad influence to predjudice or distemper their minds. I have advised them to return as soon as they can after they have suitably expressed their duty and respect to you, as I should be sorry they should lose more time from their Studies than shall be needful and also as they will likely have occasion to take several other Journeys soon after their return. I wish your Honor the Divine Presence, Direction and Blessing in the Important Business Providence has assigned you in Life and beg leave to assure you that I am with much Esteem and Respect,

Your Honor's most obedient and very humble servant,

ELEAZER WHEELOCK.

Sir Wm. Johnson, Baronet.

Sʳ William Johnson Barᵗ
Major General of the English Forces in North America

Bradford's celebrated Press, even then unobtainable and now of great value as one of the rarest of American books.

Although his treaties with them showed the concession of great grants of unoccupied territory to the King's domain, he protected them in their occupancies and reserved rights with a jealous care, which would afford a model for later "Indian Agencies." He carried into effect the policy which Governor Dongan had foreshadowed, of keeping the control of the Indians on British soil and protecting them from the zealous Missionary efforts of their French neighbors, to consolidate them with their own tribes.

Like Lord Chatham, he died in harness, devoting his last hours to duty. The progress of prospecting for locations on Indian lands was already active in 1774. Captain Michael Cresap and Mr. Greathead, had by attendant ravages in the valley of the Ohio, on lands protected by Treaty obligations, aroused Logan and other chiefs, friendly to the whites. It was the old story, with which we have been familiar from youth, being repeated. The entire Indian race on the continent sympathized, the Six Nations were preparing to take arms, even Johnson trembled at the prospect. He invited them to a Great Council, and appealed to their old relations as a guarantee for justice. Sick, when he entered the council, he vehemently addressed them, as was his custom, and died before the session was completed — on the eleventh of July, 1774, in his sixtieth year; but his parting words carried their wonted influence, and peace was preserved.

He combined some of the characteristics of Nestor with those of Ulysses, and surely presents in his administration of his public trust and mainly in his private life, an example to those charged with large duties and responsibilities. In the plentitude of his evidences of his master's favor and the pressing variety of his occupations, it is doubtful whether in the growing disfavor for the taxes on stamps or tea, he found time even to consider the reasons for a change of government, or felt that a seat in Parliament would have increased his own importance or representative control.[14]

It is no reflection upon the purity of the motives, or the wisdom of the action of the fathers of our country that such cases of those thus personally impressed with other views, should have existed, but it is merely another instance of the sometimes honest diversity of opinion and policy which has made the world a battle field.

It may be assumed that then as now, men were governed by individuality and subordinated all to the duty of loyalty, combined in such cases with a sense of interest; and one can easily see how possessing all they could hope for, both father and son struggled to retain it, as would now the holder of a similar valuable estate, franchise, or monopoly, against legislative absorbtion, opposing opinion, or even suggested amendment.

We see, even in the peaceful walks of life, one man of otherwise noble character, loose self control in asserting a grievance or supporting a right against another, where both are honest, and one, inevitably wrong. Such material, when aggregated even for social purposes, will at times divide in sentiment, and struggle in a ballot, to decide what is humane or right or what is regular, and by the vote of the majority, produce a result in suppressing without altering a deeply seated conviction.

[14] It does not appear that he ever revisited England, as was asserted, but it *may* be recalled that he was the first white man — borne by the Indians on a litter — who resorted to the "Saratoga Springs" for medicinal relief.

Such differences are apparently but miniature representations of the elements aggregated in civil war. A reference to a disinterested party has often remedied the one as a mediation may avoid the other.

John Bright, that life long advocate of peace, who has lived through many wars, has recently presented a remedy against their recurrence. "The policy and aspect of our country and of the world will be changed, if the demon war is confined to the cases in which there seems to Christian and rational men no escape from the miseries it inflicts on mankind." This seems a glittering generality only, until it can be discovered *how* the passion and perhaps the ignorance by which it is generally incited can be induced — best before any use of violence — to submit to such proper arbitration, and then *who* would be admitted to be "rational men" by any usual method of selection.

At least the position of those who sustained the existing government at the Revolution would not appear to have been open to any such solution. A large body of the people had finally settled upon a new form, to which all must submit, without reference to former complication, interest, or ties. There was no intermediate course, nor opportunity to temporize, especially for one prominent from position.

The "Tory" then fought for his sovereign and the existing laws, often after years of resistance to their exactions in every appeal but that of arms, as distasteful then as now. The conservative element had favored to the last, endurance to contest, of which property and business were to bear the cost. Many, even of the leading patriots of the Revolution during its progress gave their testimony, that they did not at its outset contemplate separation, but only to urge concession by the threat supported by force; some of them favored mutual conciliation to the end, most prayed for peace.

We have been educated to consider the action of those who were satisfied with the existing government in 1776, as well as that of those who had realized and sought for peaceful redress from grievances, and when they culminated in war adhered to their old flag, indiscriminately, as absolutely indefensible; to apply to all of them the epithet "Tory," as equivalent to "Traitor," and to forget that the even worse detested " Hessian " was only an involuntary German soldier in jackboots and bearded, then unusual in America, whose sword was again sold under treaty obligations, by his Hereditary Prince to a kinsman, King George III, in that war. We have not cared to recognize his hostility to us as compulsory, his presence that of the involuntary victim of an obnoxious custom in the old World, and that he was of the same race—and if an officer, of its educated and then privileged class—famed from the period of Charlemagne in the battle fields of the world, for their achievements, among the more recent of which we can now recall their instrumentality—including the death of two Princes of Brunswick—in the earlier conflicts, in the overthrow of two Emperors of the Bonaparte dynasty, and its suppression.

The Tory was not allowed to remain after the Revolution had succeeded, to submit to the result of what he had from habit and education rejected, when pressed upon him by arms.

It would seem to be improper, after the expiration of a century, to question the action of the brave men—carefully selected to represent the popular sentiment, and clearly influenced by more than usual intelligence—as to their policy in the smallest detail, in securing our national existence, or to believe that they could have acted in this important particular, without a better knowledge than we can even yet appreciate, of their position and of their necessities.

We know that our country was exhausted in men and means when the contest ended,[15] that the British lion had retreated

---

[15] The following copied from a signed duplicate original, shows the necessity of the government, the relative ability of the States, and the changes in their subsequent progress.

BY THE UNITED STATES, IN CONGRESS ASSEMBLED.

September 4, 1782.

On the report of a General Committee, consisting of a member from each state,

Resolved, That one million two hundred thousand dollars has been quotaed on the States as absolutely and immediately necessary for payment of the interest on the public debt; and that it be recommended to the Legislatures of the respective States, to lay such taxes as shall appear to them most proper and effectual for immediately raising their quota of the above sum.

Resolved, That the money so raised in each State, shall be applied towards paying the interest due on certificates issued from the loan office of each State, and other liquidated debts of the United States contracted therein, before any part thereof shall be paid into the public treasury.

Ordered, That the foregoing Resolutions be referred to the Grand Committee, to *assess and report* the quota of each State.

Sept. 10, 1782.

On the report of the Grand Committee:

Resolved, That $1,200,000 to be raised for the payment of the interest of the domestic debt of the United States, be appropriated to the several States, according to the following quotas, viz:

New Hampshire,	$48,000
Massachusetts,	192,000
Rhode Island,	28,800
Connecticut,	133,200
New York,	54,000
New Jersey,	66,000
Pennsylvania,	180,000
Delaware,	16,800
Maryland,	132,000
Virginia,	174,000
North Carolina,	88,800
South Carolina,	72,000
Georgia,	14,400
	$1,200,000

(Signed), CHAS. THOMPSON, *Secretary.*

grimly, still holding his Canadian territory as a lair, which could be used after the repose he also needed, as a base for the concentration of another effort, perhaps including the Loyalists and exchanged Hessian prisoners. That the private contributions made in England to aid the government, after the capture of Burgoyne, might be renewed and concert increased, after the surrender of Cornwallis, inspired by national chagrin. They perhaps felt that a Preliminary Peace wrung from a mortified enemy, was really a truce, depending on England's adjustment of her difficulties with France. That the forces of that ally, had hurried the attack upon Yorktown, to seek new laurels in the West Indies, and might never return, and that even Definitive Treaties had often been broken.

Even after that Peace, they probably doubted its continuance — as was justified by the war of 1812 [16] — and from these considerations, looked upon the continued presence of the Tory element as likely to prove a lasting danger.

A reference to "Sabine's Loyalists" will readily show, in the records of many of them in the Colonial and Revolutionary wars, that they were largely men of military experience [17] and the ques-

[16] In his "Campaigns of the War of 1812 and 15," recently published, General Cullum — who will be remembered by posterity for his life labor in recording the military records of all of the graduates of the military academy — throws much light on a dark subject. Intending to do justice to the officers of his own — the Engineer corps, he has apparently afforded the best account of the strategic failure of a war gallantly fought in the field, but so disgracefully managed in the Bureau, as to leave an impression, in many competent minds, that it was intended to be a failure, to avoid the annexation of Canada, then by reason of the scarcity of British Troops and other circumstances apparently possible.

[17] The "Letters from the Marquis de Montcalm, Governor General of Canada, &c.," published by Almon, in London, in 1777, in the heat of the controversy — and at once declared, even in Parliament, to contain predictions manufactured after the results were verified — are still a subject of discussed authenticity, although mainly settled by recent developments by Francis Parkman and others, to have been simulated. At least they appear to contain a valuable cotemporary view of the condition of the then Colonies, the material of their population, and the probability of their speedily turning their arms against their mother country, when the danger of the French as a hostile neighbor was removed.

tion for the victors to pass upon, was whether a cordial acceptance of the result of their recent overthrow could be relied upon, and a new allegiance could divest them of their old attachment or entirely subordinate them to the impressions and duties, necessary to reliable citizenship.

It has been claimed, that as they included in their number many large holders of property, and that its forfeiture — on which new fortunes were speedily founded — the release of debts and arrears before the war, to, and the cancelling of contracts with them, were also used as influences against an amnesty on even severe conditions,[18] such as had usually then been extended to the Indians, after their conquest, by most of the colonies.

It was said by Addison, that "a man of merit in a different principle, is like an object seen in two different mediums, that appears crooked and broken, however straight and entire it may be in itself. For this reason there is scarcely *a person of figure* in England, who does not go by two contrary characters, as opposite to one another as light and darkness."

[18] The severity of an indiscriminate confiscation was early recognized. In the preliminary Treaty of Peace, formulated at Versailles on the 20th of January, 1783, negotiated by Adams, Franklin, Jay and Henry Laurens, on the part of the United States — all illustrious citizens and principally foreign ministers — the only representative of Great Britain was Richard Oswald, a merchant of London, selected alone to represent her, without the ceremony attending happier negotiations and probably with a view to his acceptability to those he was to meet, as having lately bailed Mr. Laurens from the Tower when captured at sea, on his way to his Mission at the Hague. By that Treaty, condensed in nine brief stipulations, in Article v, "It is agreed that the Congress shall earnestly recommend it to the Legislatures of the respective States, to provide for the restitution of all estates, rights and properties of persons resident in districts, in the possession of his Majesty's arms, and who have not borne arms against the said United States. And that persons, of any other description, shall have free liberty to go into any part or parts of any of the Thirteen United States, and therein to remain twelve months unmolested in their endeavors to obtain the restitution of each of their estates, rights and properties, as may have been confiscated; and that Congress shall also earnestly recommend to the several states

It may be noticed that the persons here incidentally alluded to, may be mostly classed as persons of figure at the period and that Addison's impression was as applicable to the colonies as to the mother country. The customs of the one had been early introduced into the other, in the habits of life, and the adoption of many of the ideas and principles which governed at home.

The acquisition of land has been as we know, from the earliest period one of the most marked instincts of man. None knew better than the settlers the traditional influence attending land secured by entail, as the basis of the perpetuation of families at home, and many younger sons and connections of such privileged owners were then amongst the first comers. Nor were they slow after their arrival in seeking for similar endowments. A vast area of readily productive land, forests, fisheries and mines, lay open to new colonists; and facile governors, sent generally by favor, to better their estates — at least before dissensions demanded more efficient selections — were ready to promote grants of crown lands, and even manors with some

a reconsideration and revision of the acts and laws regarding the premises, so as to render the said laws or acts perfectly consistent, not only with justice and equity, but with the spirit of conciliation, which on the return of the blessings of peace should universally prevail. And that Congress shall also earnestly recommend to the several States, that the estates, rights and properties of such last mentioned persons, shall be restored to them, they refunding to any persons who may be now in possession, the bona fida price (where any has been given) which such persons may have paid on purchasing any of said lands or properties, since the confiscation. And it is agreed, That all persons who have any interest in confiscated lands, either by debts, marriage settlements, or otherwise, shall meet with no legal impediment in the prosecution of their just rights." It was also agreed by Article vi. "That there shall be no future confiscations made, nor any prosecutions commenced against any person or persons for, or by reason of the part which he or they may have taken in the present war, and that no person shall, on that account, suffer any future loss or damage, either in his person, liberty or property, and that those who may be in confinement on such charge at the time of the ratification of the Treaty in America, shall be immediately set at liberty, and the prosecution so commenced be discontinued."

feudal privileges, induced by the eking out of a small salary by the considerable fees attending the entries, and often,— as existing written evidence proves — by a concealed interest with the grantee. To the foundation of such granted or purchased estates followed their division and use by tenants, or distribution by sale. There were many monopolies, similarly procured, soon also available as sources of wealth and as the crops and productions of the land, the mines, the timber, the naval stores, and the fisheries increased, and their development and control by merchants and shippers accumulated wealth, there followed naturally the introduction of every luxury and appliance, custom and habit of life, used by the privileged class in the mother country.

The military and civil service brought out many cadets of English families, to find a permanent home by settlement or marriage. As England was politically an aristocracy, the colonies as a part of it, imitated its habits and fostered its restrictions. It has been claimed that with many who had acquired the convexity of affluence, and aspired to position, the exclusion from the higher offices, and the precedence on a state occasion, accorded to some stripling subaltern in a crimson coat, was a grievance harder to be borne than taxation. With prosperity and wealth came the desire for education, and that cultivation which should confer on their children some of the advantages which they had seen accorded, to the scions of those privileged families at home.

The schools of Eton and Harrow, and the Universities of Oxford and Cambridge, were filled with young Americans, who, while studying the humanities, were naturally comparing the political privileges which surrounded them, with those of their home.

Those in London, during the period of the dissensions referred to, watched the progress of events in the galleries of Parliament and studied statesmanship there, often with their profession in the purlieus of the Temple and the Inns of Court, both indispensible in the coming events in that distant home. Probably in their social intercourse they felt the sense of inferiority as colonists, impressed upon them by the home-born young Britons, ever conscious of national and often of personal superiority — with whom they were associated, and already dreamed of political and social equality.[19]

Their home constituency, combining a large element of veterans taught to wield arms in the border wars, conscious of their power; and of those devoted to the pursuits of peace, conceded in the selection for such offices as were left to their choice, the claims of superior education and larger opportunity for the study of public affairs; for in those days, the place sought the man as generally as in the present, men seek the place. As an example, Edward Rutledge, Thomas Hayward, Jr., Thomas Lynch, Jr., and Arthur Middleton, all early movers for redress from grievances, members from South Carolina of the early Congresses, and its Signers of the Declaration,

[19] An amusing instance of the social line then drawn, is given by Col. Stone. When William, an half breed — supposed to be Sir William's boy, and an associate of young Brant at Dr. Wheelock's school, was directed by his instructor's son to saddle a horse, he refused, saying *he was not a Gentleman*. When asked to define what a gentleman was, he replied, " a person who keeps race horses and drinks Madeira wine, and that is what neither you nor your father do." It is not probable that this impression originated with the boy, but it suggests whether the keeping of too many race horses, and the drinking of too much Madeira, may not have been one of the causes of the distinction he describes finding its decadence in the progress of events and the development of new elements of citizenship, rapidly dividing property and power with these earlier comers.

were, with Charles Coatesworth Pinckney, John Laurens and many others early in the field from that, and a large number who served in both from other Colonies — recently educated in England.

The Congress that declared the country free, which was probably as representative of the ability of the American people as any that succeeded it, was, according to the custom of the day, composed of such " men of figure " in the colonies as the people at the time, considered best suited to protect their common interest. The Clergy, Lawyers, Doctors, Judges, Magistrates, Planters and prosperous Merchants and Manufacturers were mainly its material; there was an entire absence of those who devoted themselves to politics or agitation professionally.

Perhaps the difference of sentiment, which soon divided the people in arms, may be illustrated by hastily referring to the career of one member of that celebrated body, who, while occupying in many particulars the same position as the Johnsons, was overwhelmed and mainly forgotten in the ruin he brought upon himself, in the honest assertion of antipodal convictions.

Richard Stockton, of New Jersey, would appear to have been symmetrically, in every relation, such a " person of figure." Born at Princeton, in 1730, on the extended estate of his fathers, carefully educated as his position justified, and his natural abilities made easy, he graduated at Nassau Hall, in 1748, under the tutelage of President Burr. When fitted by professional training, he readily asserted his position, as one of the ablest of a distinguished bar. The cultivation of his mind, is said to have kept pace with that of a graceful and attractive person, physically fitted for endurance and superiority in all manly enterprises. While doing the honors of his stately home, with a broad hospitality and benevolence, aided by a wife to whom he was devoted, he had adorned it with many objects of interest, including one of the finest libraries in the colonies.

He combined an interest in all that affected the public, with an appreciation of every social pleasure, uniting in the gayeties of the little Viceregal Court of his Governor, Sir William Franklin,[20] while already considering the grievances charged against his delegated action. He is claimed by his honorable character, and sympathetic manners, to have earned the appreciation of all. Devoting his leisure to the improvement of his mind, body and estate, on the latter he bred the choicest horses and cattle, he was celebrated for his mount as well as for his seat, for his skill as a marksman, and in such

---

[20] Governor Franklin was a protege of Lord Bute, by whose influence and that of his father — when courted by the administration — he was created Governor of New Jersey without any marked service above that of a captain in the French War. On his release he returned to Europe. His more memorable father who could control lightning failed in influencing the loyalty of his son.

In many particulars there was a similarity between the position and treatment of Governor Franklin and Sir John Johnson in this year. The following letter is copied from the original and shows the action of Congress.

PHILADELPHIA, *June* 24, 1776.

GENTLEMEN: Your Favor respecting the proper measures to be taken with your late Governor, William Franklyn, Esq., came to Hand on Saturday the 22d inst. But as the Congress did not sit on that Day I could not lay it before them till Monday. I now do myself the Honour of enclosing to you the Resolve of Congress which they have this day passed with Regard to the Treatment of him. You will therefore perceive the Congress have directed him to be sent to Connecticut under a guard. I shall write to Gov. Trumbull to treat him as a Prisoner should he refuse to give his Parole in Writing.

I have the Honour to be Gentlemen your most
obed't and very humble serv't.
JOHN HANCOCK,
Presid't.

The other resolves herewith transmitted, are of such a Nature that no arguments are necessary to enforce them. You will be pleased to attend to them as soon as possible.

Hon'ble Convention of New Jersey.

athletic sports as are now supplemented by polo, lawn tennis, boating and ball matches, in which pleasure is realized through exertion. Such pursuits and pastimes of his lesser existence, were with him only the oil applied to the machinery of an earnest life!

In 1766, he "made his tour," as was customary then as now, spending two years in England, cultivating the acquaintance of public men to whom his access was easy, obtaining an audience by the young King, who graciously received him, and communing with some leaders, with whom he was destined to hold early intercourse, and to whom he, even then, probably imparted his growing apprehensions. In an unpublished letter, written in London in that year to his wife — one of the few relics of his then impending ruin, which survive in the hands of his family, and which Dr. Emmet thoughtfully directed to be fac-similed — he says, " I have had a perfect state of health since I left you, blessed be God Almighty, and let me tell you that all the Elegance and Grandeur I have yet seen in these Kingdoms, in different families where I have been received, serves but to increase the pleasure I have for some years enjoyed in my Domestick connections. I see not a sensible, obliging, tender wife, but the Image of my dear Emelia, is full in view. I see not a haughty ignorant imperious dame, but I rejoice that the partner of my life is so much her opposite. But why need I talk so gallantly? You knew me long ago, as well as you would should I write a volume on this endearing topic."

The fitness of a man so constituted and prepared for public usefulness, was not then long overlooked. Returning in 1768, he was named for a seat in the Council of the colony—

at the time an honored place, and, in 1774, elevated to the Supreme Bench, acquitting himself with credit in each position. When he saw the political clouds which he had carefully watched, about to break, he had prepared himself by study of precedents, and communion with wise men, for the result, and made every effort to avert it. The annexed appeal, copied from the original draft — written with a firm and graceful chirography, but in ink as faded by time as any general memory of his service — expressing the result of such conclusion in dignified and manly terms, and showing by its impersonal form, the writer's appreciation of the etiquette, which prevented a direct interference with public affairs beyond his control — was submitted to the minister without concealment of authorship or the avoidance of responsibility, by the hand of a friend."

" AN EXPEDIENT FOR THE SETTLEMENT OF THE AMERICAN DISPUTES humbly submitted ("offered" erased) to the consideration of his Majesty's Ministers, by an American.

The State of American Affairs is so badly alarming at this time, that any real friend to the British Empire, ought to suggest every probable expedient that occurs to him, for the accommodation of the unhappy disputes between Great Britain and the Colonies — to give the following suggestions their due weight, it must be premised— 1st. That the several North American Colonies, from New Hampshire to South Carolina inclusive, *are able to furnish* 500,000 *fighting men ;* who are in general as fit for service as the English Militia, and many of them much more so, having been in active service in the last war. 2nd. That the great body of the people of these several Colonies are now (even to the astonishment of many Colonists themselves) *perfectly united in a determinate opposition to the authority of the British Parliament as to all internal Taxation.* 3d. That there is not the least remaining doubt, if the British Government should proceed to put the late Acts of Parliament, respecting the Massachusetts Bay (or any other Acts which involve the Idea of an absolute uncontrollable power in the British Parliament over the Colonies); into execution, by force, but that the said *Colonies would unite by attempting to repel, force by force.* To which may be added, what is as well or perhaps better known in Great Britain than in America, to wit : 4th. That the *certain* consequences of this unnatural war will be dreadful to both Great Britain and America, and the *probable* effects thereof may be fatal to the whole British Empire. Matters standing thus and the three first propositions above premised being founded upon the most indubitable facts (of which the writer of this from his general acquaintance with America, is perhaps as competent a

Such remonstrances, made in and out of Parliament by the friends of America, desirous of preserving with honor its early institutions, failed to attract attention, and the storm of opposition to them finally burst. Stockton had already selected his course and indifferent to office, personal exemption, or private

judge as any man whatever), it is humbly proposed to his Majesty's Ministers whether it would not be proper, 1st. That a royal Instruction be immediately obtained and sent over to the several Governors of the North American Colonies requesting them forthwith to recommend it to their several Assemblies to pass, and to give their own assent to an Act which may be passed by the Legislatures of several Provinces, comprising certain *Commissioners therein to be named to repair to England*, with power to confer with his Majesty's Ministers, or with Commissioners to be appointed by Parliament, respecting the grand points in dispute between Great Britain and America, and finally to determine thereupon. 2nd. That to prevent all disputes in future, the said American Commissioners be also empowered to confer and agree with the British Commissioners respecting the *future Government and regulation of the Colonies*, either by framing one general system of Government for all the Colonies on the Continent similar to the British, or by making some material alteration in the present mode of Provincial Government. *In either* of which systems, some effectual provision may be made *for the adequate support of the American Government by the Americans themselves*, and also for the payment of all such sums of money as may become due from America to Great Britain for the assistance of her Fleets and Army. These determinations of the said Commissioners to be subjected nevertheless, to such alteration as the wisdom of his Majesty and his Parliament of Great Britain may make therein, and as shall be agreed to by the several Provincial Legislatures. 3d. That upon such instructions being given to the several Governors, his Majesty to be advised in his royal clemency, to recommend it to his Parliament to *suspend the operation of the Boston Port Acts*, while the determination of the said Commissioners should be had. The author of the above hints offers them with all humility, and with great diffidence of his own ability on so great and national a question. *But some expedient must be immediately fallen upon, or we shall be involved in a Civil War, the most obstinate, awful and tremendous that perhaps ever occurred since the Creation of the World.* He will esteem it a signal blessing of Divine Providence conferred upon him, if any one Idea he hath suggested may be of any use at this *dreadful crisis.* And if otherwise, he will at least be able to comfort himself with the uprightness of his intentions in this feeble attempt, and with the assurance that he can do no harm, either to himself or any other person.

December 12, 1774.

Endorsed by the writer — on this the corrected draught — "Hints transmitted to Lord Dartmouth, Secretary of State for America, through the hands of Samuel Smith, Esq., of London, Merchant."

This Appeal, and many similar ones we know, were made in vain to a government impressed by unwise counsels, and a King who declared "That the Americans meant only to amuse by vague expressions of attachment and the strongest professions

interest, accepted a seat in the *then* rebel Congress. While the Declaration of Independence was being considered, he listened in silence, and with profound attention to the debate, but with a grave face and a sad heart,[22] when under later usages, a member who had determined to risk his life for the benefit of his "constituency," might have suggested some trifling amendment, to remind them at once of his presence at an important crisis, and the superior grasp of his intellect to that of the illustrious committee who reported it. It has been suggested that the Congress of 1776, was limited in its membership to men whose merit had been recognized in the administration of their own private interests and duties, a valued experience to those assuming a public trust. Many of them had shown this also in the colonial assemblies, where the honor had compensated for the expense, beyond the trifling allowance. When the proper moment arrived he signed it, accepted it as the chart by which he was fated to sail to his personal shipwreck, overwhelmed while aiding to secure the privileges we enjoy.

In devoting himself to the cause, he declined the honors offered to him, to compensate for those he had sacrificed. On a tie vote, between himself and William Livingston — another devoted and able patriot — on the first election for governor, he declined further contest with so worthy a man, and also refused the Chief Justiceship, probably won by his magnanimity. With

of loyalty, while they were preparing for a general revolt, for the purpose of establishing an independent Empire." At least, the policy suggested by Mr. Stockton had some influence at home, for on the first day of the following September, Richard Penn and Arthur Lee delivered to Lord Dartmouth a petition from Congress to the King embodying the above views and probably borrowed from them, and were informed that NO ANSWER WOULD BE GIVEN.

[22] Sanderson's Signers.

his colleague Clymer, he visited the camp of the Northern army, and consulted with the gallant Schuyler, as to details already tending there to a great triumph. Soon, the ravages of war reached and destroyed that happy home, his family was driven into exile, his lands were laid waste, and his favorite horses appropriated by the raiders. Then, to complete his misfortunes, when captured by them, he was carried into New York, and from his prominent position as a recent King's officer, "ignominiously thrown into a common jail," and confined with such cruelty that when exchanged, upon the special remonstrances of Congress, conveyed by Washington, his shattered health unfitted him for further usefulness, and a lingering life of suffering was the final fulfillment of his remarkable promise, which terminated on the twenty-eighth of February, 1781, too soon to know of the effect of the artillery at Yorktown, in consummating the freedom for which, after exhorting his children to remember that "the fear of God is the beginning of wisdom," he had died a martyr. In many countries such service would be recorded by monuments "more lasting than brass," and his "fetê day" remembered and celebrated; in the engrossing present of what he aided to create, is it not doubtful if his name is known to all of those even in his native State, where some evidently concentrate in themselves and in their surroundings, the beginning and end of all interest in the perpetuation of their existence as freemen. Is it not equally so, if he were living, whether those services would command a sufficient vote of appreciation to return him to Congress, if vigorously opposed by some political organization or machine, supported by the now common outlay.

But our national existence appears largely due to the folly of its rulers, even more than to the resistance of the colonies. When relieved of a hostile neighbor by the conquest of Canada, they needed no longer the protecting assistance of the parent government. The continuous border warfare with the French then ended, and also that with all of the Indians, surrounding the upper lakes, in the successful defence of Detroit and the defeat of Pontiac. During the continuance of these wars, they had been compelled to keep an average of 25,000 troops under arms, and had made a valuable expenditure of thirty thousand lives. They claimed a large balance, some £350,000 for outlays. A vote of £200,000 by Parliament on the recommendation of George III at once on his accession, while admitting the necessity for such assistance, seems inconsistent with a claim soon after made for a revenue of £100,000 by direct taxation. In 1775 the debt of Great Britain was estimated at three hundred millions and its interest charges in 1776, £4,800,000 of which £19,000 was claimed as for the expenses of the first year of the war.

There had been dissensions between the Governors and the Assemblies, and a successful resistance to the foreign taxes on sugar and molasses. Writs of assistance ordering the collection, had been reluctantly granted, and little used. An uncomfortable relation had grown up between the colonies, now a prosperous and warlike people, and their mother country. Sir Robert Walpole[23] had years before divined that their direct taxation was

[23] Doubtless their clandestine trade with the Spanish Colonies, exporting British manufactures in exchange for specie, made stamps more objectionable, but far seeing Walpole claimed, that of every £500,000 so gained by them, one-half would be expended in England. Their friends throughout persistently sustained them in Parliament. Chatham, Rockingham, Newcastle, Camden and Conway amongst the earliest, with such success, that when partially to aid the East India Company, three pence a pound on tea was, on motion of Lord North alone persisted in, — on the 5th of March, 1770 — Captain Preston had on that day, fired on the "Boston Mob," and the concession came too late.

to "disturb a hornets' nest," and left it as he said — as many political questions are bequeathed — "to those who should come after him, who had more courage than himself;" and the judicious Pitt, when it was suggested as a source of needed revenue, expressed his unwillingness to "burn his fingers with an American Tax." What the course of events would have been, if Frederick, Prince of Wales, had lived to succeed his father, is a subject for conjecture. He appears to have been controlled by generous impulses, and advanced ideas of government, was frank and ingenuous in his carriage, while doubtless a subject for "calculation" or at least observation as to his future, as an heir apparent of mature years is apt to be. It was asserted that he favored dividing the control of his father's Whig advisors — representing the ruling party since the Protestant succession — and admitting the long neglected Tory element to share it, and to neutralize the influence of both, by subordinating every element to the development, in his expected reign—of Bolingbroke's ideal government, ruled by a "*Patriot King.*" Dying in his father's lifetime, at the age of forty-four, his son succeeded directly on the decease of his grandfather on the 26th of October, 1760, at the age of twenty-two, having been the first of his family born on British soil.

The accession of George III[24] to the throne *when proclaimed throughout his dominions and colonies*, was received every where

---

[24] It was said of him at that time "though his character was far from yet being perfectly developed, a very strong and apparently just partiality predominated in his favor. During the late reign he had uniformly abstained from all public interference in the affairs of government. His manners were in the highest degree decorous, his words unblemished, and his personal accomplishments corresponded with the elevation of his rank and station. All appearances seemed to augur a reign of uninterrupted glory and felicity, and the regret which the nation for a moment felt at the sudden demise of the good old King, was immediately absorbed in the transports of joy excited by the auspicious commencement of the reign of the young Monarch who

with demonstrations of hope and joy. The people mainly at last, attached to his family, augured from his character and youth, a relief from every existing complication. Their grievances and prayers for redress were early addressed to the new monarch, and steadily pressed on his attention, with increasing emphasis. The hand of his mother—a Princess who was known by the populace as " The Witch," and doubtless held herself to be capable and executive—seems to have shaped his destiny as woman has often influenced the destinies of mankind. His father, apparently no mean judge of character, speaking of John Stewart, Earl of Bute, whom he had first seen at the Duchess of Queensbury's fete, acting as "Lothario" in the "Fair Penitent," apparently soon as an intimate at Leicester House, epigrammatically described him as "a fine showy man who would make an excellent ambassador in any court, where there was no business" (Beeton's Universal Biography), and all his-

had very lately attained the age of complete majority; being born June 4, 1738." *Belsham's Memoirs of George III.*

The late Dean Stanley, in his "Memorials of Westminster Abbey," recalls some details of the coronation of George III, that Archbishop Secker who officiated, had baptized, confirmed and married, the King. That the princely style in which the young King seated himself after the ceremony, attracted general notice." "No actor in the character of Pyrrhus, in the 'Distrest Mother,'" says Bishop Newton, who was present, "not even Booth himself, ever ascended the throne with so much grace and dignity." That the most interesting peculiarity of the coronation was the unnoticed attendance of the rival to the throne, Prince Charles Edward" (the Pretender, then in London, under the name of Mr. Brown). "I asked my Lord Marshal," says David Hume, "the reason for this strange fact." "Ay," says he, "a gentleman told me so, who saw him there, and whispered in his ear, ' Your Royal Highness is the last of all mortals whom I should expect to see here." "It was curiosity that led me," said the other, "but I assure you," added he, "that the person who is the cause of all this pomp and magnificence, is the man I envy least." Could he have realized what that rival would soon suffer from the losses here treated of, he would not have envied him the more, on that day that he inherited those troubles, with the preferment.

The signature of Archbishop Secker, who aided and endowed Episcopal churches in America, and also officiated at the coronation of Lord Granville, Dunk, Earl of Halifax, and others of the Lords of Council annexed to the order for his proclamation in New York, like that of Goldsboro Banyer, the then Deputy Secretary, may be recalled in connection with our early history.

torians appear to agree in failing to approve of the man. He was, says Belsham — apparently an impartial writer — "a nobleman haughty in his manners, contracted in his capacity, despotic in his sentiments, and mysterious in his conduct, who was successfully insinuating himself into the confidence of the Princess of Wales, and of her son." Only Sunday intervened between the old King's death, and his taking his oath as a Privy Counsellor, and he at once supplanted his daughter, Princess Amelia, in the Rangership of Richmond Park.[25] As the Mentor of the Prince he became a rapid meteor, shooting upward from place to place, from that position to Secretary of State, then to first Lord of the Treasury, and ruler of the Ministry of the Nation, of the Princess Dowager, and of his Sovereign. The latter had learned to thoroughly accept his infallibility and to adopt his ideas, which culminated in his misfortunes, and loss of colonies and intellect. Lord Bute drove from the counsels of his well intending master, all other advisers, including those apparently essential to his prosperity. Some refused to serve as his colleagues, others were supplanted in securing place and emolument for himself and his creatures. While in thus depriving America of friends in the Council, familiar with their rights and necessities, he concentrated power in himself. It is just to say, that he pressed the war against the Allies on the continent, with vigorous success, on sea and land, bringing them to their knees, and negotiating the Peace of Fontainbleau in November, 1762, with France, Spain and Portugal, by which Canada and all Louisiana east of Mississippi was finally ceded, by France; East and West Florida and all their territory east and south-east of that river, by Spain. In the haste with which he availed himself of these successes, securing the results which made

[25] Possibly to please her sister-in-law.

the "Georgian Era" memorable, he immensely increased the area of the colonies. He neglected to provide any indemnity for Prussia as a faithful ally, from her position liable to future retaliation, and won those caustic, but just criticisms with which that Frederick, who was *great* with both pen and sword — after having protected his then exposed condition by a treaty with Russia and Sweden, has embalmed his memory in his *Œuvres du Roi de Prusse*. This, and the forcing through with great difficulty, even sustained by the whole power of the Government, of the "Cider Bill," involving a direct tax repugnant to the whole people, especially to the "Country Party," and the agricultural interests, and so establishing a precedent for those which cost the recent acquisitions in America, and their base, were the crowning results of a power which he suddenly resigned, when—as he admitted "single in a Cabinet of his own creating, with no soul in the House of Lords to support him, but two Peers." All of this unwise exercise of authority appears to have originated in the Princess Dowager's rejection, of what the world have since united in approving, as the wise judgment of her husband, and allowing the needy schemer he distrusted, the unrestricted control of that of his son, particularly on this to him, fatal question of direct taxation.

William Henry Drayton — Chief Justice of South Carolina — who was in the habit of engrafting ardent precepts of patriotism with those of law, in his charges to the grand jury and also of contributing his salary to their promotion,[26] expressed the universal sense of the Colonies in one of these delivered on the 15th of October, 1776.

"Never were a people more wrapped up in a King than the Americans were in George III in 1763. They revered

---

[26] He also died in service, a member of Congress at Philadelphia, Feb. 3, 1779.

and obeyed the British Government because it protected them, they fondly called Great Britain *home*, but from that time her counsels took a ruinous turn; ceasing to protect they sought to ruin America, the Stamp Act, Declaratory law and duties upon Tea and other articles, at once proclaimed the injustice, and announced to Americans that they had but little room for hope, infinite space for fear. In vain they petitioned for redress."

But England needed money; and the means as proposed to the King, by Bute, seemed to him adequate and proper. In an effort to add to her revenue the £100,000, Mr. Grenville[27] his successor as first Commissioner of the Treasury, proposed to collect it by the Stamp Act in 1763, and so partially reimburse her outlay in the Seven Years' War, which had in part originated in the defence of her Colonies. In this she thoroughly aroused them, already exasperated, to a forcible resistance, so significant as to strengthen the hands of its opponents in Parliament sufficiently to effect the repeal of that already obsolete act.

Even then there was a chance for reconciliation, for which the Colonies still steadily petitioned and labored through their agents and friends. But the fumes of the "Cider Bill" had influenced the royal head, he persevered in his policy, and the brilliant Charles Townshend, as Chancellor of the Exchequer,

[27] In the course of the debate on the Cider Bill, Mr. Grenville, annoyed by Mr. Pitt's ridicule of its subject, replied, "The Right Honorable Gentleman complains of the hardship of this Tax; why does he not tell us where we can lay another tax instead of it?" repeating two or three times emphatically, "Tell me *where* you can lay another tax." Mr. Pitt thus unseasonably appealed to, replied in a musical tone, in the words of a favorite air, "Gentle Shepherd tell me where," which, amused the House and fixed the soubrequet on Mr. Grenville. Mr. Belsham, who related it in 1795, did not view it even then as wholly a joke. "Little certainly," says he, "did this minister imagine how fertile would be the invention of his successors, or how thuroughly subdued by time and custom the spirits of the people." This tax, however, was also soon obsolete from *non usor*.

four years later essayed to increase the still insufficient revenue, by the substitution of a more remunerative duty upon tea, glass, paper and painters' colors, under the impression that the form and not the substance of the taxation was unpalatable, but even when limited to tea alone, its attempted enforcement was, as we know, the immediate cause of the loss of her Colonies, at least at that time.

It was a small beginning to a mighty result, the spark that caused a great conflagration, in which, in spite of the efforts of Lord North, into whose hands and those of Lord George Germain,— whom Belsham emphasizes as "so famous, or rather infamous, under his former appellation of Lord George Sackville,"— after several intermediate unsuccessful ministries it fell, to make the final efforts to extinguish it by conciliation, too long delayed, or by force ; and so to officiate, in the final dismemberment of a portion of Great Britain's dominions, now vastly larger and greater, than the whole at that period. The Tory interests were then remorselessly burned.

The few details of public outlay referred to in these old papers, only valuable here as connected with the subject, are, it will be seen, trifling items of the then immense expenditure of the British Government in that fruitless struggle for a small additional Revenue, and additions to her indebtedness always very great, but easily carried in ordinary times by the appreciation of her Funded Debt, as a security by the world. From these fragments, we can discern the continued confidence of the Government in Sir John Johnson, after the military results elsewhere referred to, and that he was entrusted with the care and control of his former allies and neighbors, apparently as the superior of Col. Guy Johnson, on whom the Superintendency devolved at the decease of Sir William, probably so arranged in order to allow him to devote his uninterrupted attention to the care of an estate, then only second to that of Penn's in size, and to enjoy it as a landed gentleman. Perhaps, as a clear judge of character in ordinary cases, he distrusted the qualities of his son to assume the Superintendency; an impression which seems oftener to prevail with an elderly man, than that of a too high appreciation of the ability of any apparent successor. In the event, fate did not free him from the cares from which his father may have hoped to relieve him, after having himself long borne their weight.

It may be noticed that the following order providing for the relief of several corps of Loyalists belonging to General Burgoyne's Army, and other Refugees, deducts the value of provisions, issued to "said Corps of Royalists and others, between 25th October, 1777"—three months after the conclusion of the foregoing Diary—"and 24th April, 1778," and probably includes the troops it treats of, as then still under command.

Guy Carleton, Knight of the Bath, General and Commander-in-chief of his Majesty's Forces in the Province of Quebec and frontiers thereof,

You are hereby directed and required to pay or cause to be paid to Sir John Johnson, Bart., or to his assigns, the sum of six thousand four hundred and sixty seven pounds, eleven shillings and six pence, sterling dollars at four shillings and eight pence each, being the allowance made for the present relief of several corps of Royalists, belonging to General Burgoyne's army, and sundry other persons who have taken refuge in this Province from the Rebellious Colonies, as per annexed accounts. You will also deduct the sum of one thousand and twenty-four pounds, six shillings and eight pence sterling, being the amount of provisions issued to the said corps of Royalists and others, between 25th October, 1777, and 24th April, 1778.

And this, with the acquittances of the said Sir John Johnson, Bt., or his assigns, shall be your sufficient Warrant and Discharge.

Given under my hand, at Quebec, this 29th of April, 1778.

GUY CARLETON.[28]

To John Powell, Esq.,
Dy. Paymaster General,
His Majesty's forces at Quebec.

This appointment — dated five months after the virtual close of the war at Yorktown, although eight before the nego-

[28] The last English commander in-chief in her lost colonies. By escaping from captivity at Montreal in 1775, passing at night, with muffled oars, through his adversaries' forces, throwing himself into Quebec, and rallying its feeble garrison, he saved the city and deprived the adventurous Montgomery of his victory. The jealousy of Lord George Germaine is said to have confined his service to Canada, and deprived him of the command of the expedition led by Burgoyne. His loyal endurance of this slight, and his cordial assistance with the favorite of the hour, won for him Burgoyne's recorded appreciation. General Burgoyne was apparently a man of ability, and had been a successful soldier in Portugal. He was a social celebrity also, and owed his progress to family influence. His devotion to pleasure is charged to have delayed him — while in fact probably waiting for the promised coöperation of General Howe — when celerity of movement appears to have offered the only chance for either advance or escape.

It has also been claimed, mainly by those not present, that his delay near Fort Edward, to procure horses for a very heavy artillery and train, increased the need of provisions, all of which the disasters of the detachments on his flanks at Fort Stanwix and Bennington, prevented his securing, while they crippled an originally small force, to swing so far from its base. It was also asserted, that he should have held Fort Edward, prepared to advance when he had satisfactory intelligence from below, or even to retreat to Canada; an apparent answer would be, that he had but five days provisions when he yielded; inconsiderable for a siege and had no knowledge of Clinton's small supplies, sent to Albany. That the whole country encouraged by those disasters, was rising, and troops being hurried forward, while his own were daily reduced; and that he was in effect captured before he surrendered. It was only at the end of a century, that General Howe's failure to advance to his aid was accounted for, by an explanation, written at the time by Lord Shelburne, and published by his appreciative grandson, in his life in 1875, by which it appears that Lord George Germaine, also a man of pleasure, being engaged to dine in the country, signed the orders for Burgoyne, but those for Gen. Howe requiring to be rewritten, were to be sent to him, for his signature there. The packet unexpectedly sailed with only the former, and so produced the complication, while the latter were found pigeon holed in the office of that valuable public servant, years afterwards, and so America gained a battle only second in value from its results. This blunder, as many other explanations just to that officer, and perhaps the best conception of the good and

tiation of the Preliminary Peace — creating him Superintendent General of all Indians at Quebec and the frontier Provinces, including his old neighbors four of the Six Nations — might imply that his hopes as a soldier had ended, with those for the restoration of his inherited domain. The evidence however exists of his continued interests in the differences with the Indians, still occupying the territory claimed by the United States, proving his later hostility.

Sir : WHITE HALL, 18 *March*, 1782.

The King has been graciously pleased to appoint you Superintendent General, and Inspector General of the Six Nations of Indians and their Confederates and also of the

evil in his character, have also been afforded to readers by the daughters of a more fortunate General, his son Sir John Burgoyne, who are now residing in Hampton Court, in the "Political and Military Sketches" published by their inspiration, by Mr. Fonblanque in 1876. These, with the "Memoirs of the Marquis of Rockingham," edited by Lord Albemarle in 1852, "The correspondence of the Duke of Bedford and Lord Chatham," "The Evelyn's in America," contributed by J. D. Scull, Oxford, 1881, Judge Jones' "History of New York in the Revolution," and the Gates papers, contributed by Dr. T. A. Emmett to the "Magazine of American History," are all among the recent proofs of the mellowing influence of Time upon History.

There appear to be many coincidences in the career of Burgoyne and that of Gates, identified as they were in service and in eventual destiny. Both types of the conventional gentleman, brilliant and epigrammatic with the pen and audacious with the sword. Equally open to a generous impulse, the error of self appreciation and a desire for rapid glory, both based some impression of infallibility on the rules of technical education and the prestige of former service. Both appear in history fit subjects to point the moral that while success is self recording, misfortune commands its equal right to a reliable record. With probably less natural ability than either, Gen. Carleton combined with courage and decision the additional requisite of business capacity. He appears to have received in all history, that which these brilliant cotemporaries sought for and failed to achieve, as a reward for his unassuming usefulness and admitted humanity. It has been considered whether there would have been a Saratoga in our roll of victories, had that active commander led the expedition. It was his singular fortune to serve in America through the war, to hold Quebec at its outset, and surrender New York at its conclusion. After the peace he became Lord Dorchester and remained in Canada as Commander-in-Chief of the British forces. The eccentric General Charles Lee, another soldier of the school of Burgoyne and Gates, influenced by his too little faith in Washington as a soldier—after the attempt to hold Fort Washington—and too much in a sense of his own educated superiority, attempted to treat, for a hasty completion of the war, as Dr. George H. Moore has shown, with an *individuality* too intense, to conceive its exercise treasonable.

Indians in the Province of Quebec, and in the Provinces lying on the Frontiers thereof.

I am happy to inform you of this Mark of His Majesty's Favor and Confidence and as it conveys to you most authentically His Royal Approbation of your former services, it will, I am sure, impress you with the warmest Sentiments of Duty and Gratitude, and excite you to exert your utmost endeavors to render your present appointment beneficial to the Public, by establishing a strict economy through all branches of your Department, which will be the best means of recommending yourself to His Majestys future Favor and Attention. You will see by the terms of your warrant that you are to follow such Orders and instructions as you shall receive from the Commander-in-Chief of His Majestys Forces in the Provinces of Quebec, I have signified to General Haldimand His Majestys Pleasure that he should make you such Allowances for your Services and Expenses as he shall judge adequate and proper. I have therefore only to signify to you His Majestys Commands that you do with all possible expedition return to Quebec and take upon you the exercise of the very important office to which you are appointed and immediately after your arrival address yourself to General Haldimand or the Commander-in-Chief of His Majesty's Forces who will give you orders for your further proceedings, which you are in all cases to pay the most exact and punctual obedience.   Sir,   Your Most Obedient
                                                humble servant,
Sir John Johnson, Bar.[30]   W. ELLIS.[29]

But, when at this interval there arose a report, that the Americans were advancing to carry their successes into Canada, and some military movements towards the frontier — probably merely demonstrations — had given it color, we find[31] Sir Ferdi-

[29] He occupied many positions of honor and trust; was a member of the Privy Council, and of Parliament for Weymouth, and created Lord Mendip in 1794.

[30] Sir John had already performed similar duties probably with local rank. He was at this time in his thirty-sixth year.

[31] Riedesel Memoirs.

nand Haldimand, commanding in Canada, alive to the danger, communicating to Baron von Riedesel, in command at Sorel, in a letter dated Quebec, February 13, 1783, that he had despatched a messenger to the "Chevalier Johnson," to send "five or six of the most active, and expert Mohawks, to watch the road from Albany to West Point," and suggesting that he, "with his savages and light batallion, fall back a few miles, even about Point au Fer," which shows him at that date again in active service.

The one thousand pounds a year furnished him, liberal pay at that time, no doubt, if poorly compensating for his own lost revenue, attests that the outlays of his government, had not yet been checked by its reverses. We can gather from another paper, that he had been engaged at that time on picket duty, in the neighborhood of his old home, scouting, having soldiers and scouts "piloted," secreting and procuring intelligence, all incident to border expeditions, probably entrusted to him from his knowledge of localities and perhaps involving some of those inhumanities, which tradition have laid to his account. For fourteen months of this service, General Haldimand appears to have compensated him at the rate of ten shillings sterling a day, a liberal allowance also, at existing values, but implying that he was not then under regular military pay.

ACCOUNTS of contingent expenses incurred by Sir John Johnson, Baronet, on account of the Government by orders of His Excellency General Haldimand in sundry services between the 25 Dec., 1780, and the 13 March, 1782.

1781.
Aug. 5. To cash to Michael Lett and party for their Services and Expenses on a Scout to Tryon County............... £11 13 4
Sept. 10. To do. to Sergeant Haines and party for their services, etc., on a Scout to the County of Tryon............ 15 10 0

1782.

Nov. 10. To Peter Prunner, late of the Albany Bush, in the County of Tryon, for Piloting soldiers and scouts employed in the service and supplying them with Provisions between the 16th June, 1779, and the 28th September, 1782...... 36 8 0

Dec. 15. To do. to Wm. Parker, Sen., for Provisions and Surveying, and procuring Intelligence and assisting Scouts Provisions between the 15th September, 1778, and the 25th Aug., 1781...... 30

" 20. To do. to Wm. Kennedy, for sundry services in secreting and procuring intelligence and Assisting Scouts with Provisions between the 15th Sept., 1778, and the 25th Aug., 1781...... 35 15 6

To cash paid to the late Samuel McKay, Esq., for Provisions overpaid for by him for his Corps......... 39 15 6

To an allowance from his Excellency General Haldimand for Extra Service from the 28th Dec., 1780 to the 13th March, 1782, inclusive at 10s. sterling per day £222......... 237 17 1

Currency........ £406 19 5

JOHN JOHNSON.

Other papers refer merely to routine duty; in them "Molly Brant" is recalled as a pensioner, and Colonels Guy Johnson, Butler, and John Campbell, all familiar names in partisan warfare, as connected still with the government service.

Receipt of Lieut. Col. John Campbell.

RECEIVED from Sir John Johnson, Baronet, Superintendent General and Inspector General of Indian Affairs, Two Thousand and fifty-seven Pounds, Thirteen Shills and Eight pence Halifax Currency being the amount of Disbursements paid by me for the Indian Department under my direction from the 25th of March to the 24th September, 1783, per acc't and vouchers delivered to him by

JOHN CAMPBELL.

£2057 13 8 Cy.

SUBSISTENCE wanted for the Officers of the Six Nations Departments from 25 March to 24 Sept., 1783, Inclusive.

Rank	Commencing	Ending	No. of Days	Rate per day	New York £ s d	Sterling £ s d
One Col & Superintendents (Pay rec'd from the General to Dec. 24 next)......	25 March	24 Sept	184	" "	" " "	300
One Deputy in Canada.......	do	do	184	" "	" " "	100
Two Lieutenants (Clement & Magin).......	do	do	184	a dollar	147 4	
One Surgeon Mate	do	do	184	do	73 12	
One Clerk	do	do	184	6s. York Cy	55 4	
One Commissary (Moses Ibbitt) Invalided and discharged ...	do	do	184	a dollar	73 12	
One Issued as a Volunteer (John Service)	do	do	184	6s. York Cy	55 4	
One Interpreter (Le Coragine) Invalided......	do	do	184	a dollar	73 12	
Catharine Hare widow of the late Lieut Hare Pension ...	do	do	184			10
					478 0 8	279 1 4
						689 1 4

COL. GUY JOHNSON.

Amt of Lieut Col Butlers Deputy Agents return hereto annexed paid by his draft on the Superintendent General................ ... 1713 4 4

Two Thousand four hundred & 2 pounds ‡................ .... £2,402 5 8
E. E. Quebec 25 October 1783.   G. JOHNSON.
£689 1 4 Col Johnson
1713 4 4 Lt Col Butler

2402 5 8 Sterling

RECEIVED from Sir John Johnson, Baronet, his Majestys Super Intendent General & Inspector General for Indian Affairs in North America the sum of £689 1s 4d sterling for my own and a Deputys Salary, the pay of officers and others employed in his Majestys service in the Indian Department under my Superintendency, from the 25 March to 24 Sept., 1783, and I certifie that the said Sir John Johnson also pay the sum of £1713 4s 4d for the pay of Lieut. Col. Butler, Deputy Agent, that of the officers and others employed in his Majestys service in the Indian Department in the district of Niagara as per the above list &c.
G. JOHNSON,[32]
Col. & Supt. of the Six Nations.

MONTREAL, 4 *August*, 1784.

SIR : Please pay to Mr. Charles McCormick or Order Sixty Eight Pounds twelve & sixpence currency being the amount of his pay from 25 March to the 24 September 1784 as Clerk & Commissary of Indian Stores for the District of Detroit.

JOHN JOHNSON.

Mr. R. Dobie, Merchant.

£54 15s. N. Y. Currency. CATARAGUI, 20 *August*, 1784.

SIR : At sight please pay Mr. Robert Hamilton or order the sum of Fifty-four pounds fifteen shillings New York Currency being the amount of my half pay up to the 24 of last March which pass to account as per advice from,

Sir, Your very humble Servant,

EBENEZER ALLEN.

To Sir John Johnson Knt
 & Baron Knight (sic) Montreal.

Mr. Dobie will please pay the above draft.

J. JOHNSON.

For £50 Currency. MONTREAL, 20 *August*, 1784.

SIR : Please pay to Mrs. Mary Brant[33] or order Fifty pounds Halifax Currency in part of her pension from Government from 23 Oct., 83 & 22 Sept. 1784.

JOHN JOHNSON.

To Mr. Richard Dobie, Montreal.

[32] Col. Guy Johnson, nephew, son-in-law, some time secretary and named as successor to Sir William Johnson.
[33] The widow of Joseph Brant [Thayendanegea] who survived her husband thirty years.

LONDON, *Dec.* 24, 1784.

Received from Sir John Johnson, Baronet, His Majestys Superintendent General and Inspector General of Indian Affairs in North America, Three Hundred Pounds Sterling for my Salary as Superintendent of the Six Indian Nations and their Allies from 25 June to the 24 Dec., 1784, Inclusive.

£300. G. JOHNSON,[34]
Col. & Superintendent of the Six Nations.

A letter from Major General Hope, Commander-in-Chief &c., to Sir John is apparently interesting, as throwing further light on a restless escapade, which is referred to in the life of that early representative of the possibilities and effect of education, even upon a savage mind. He had determined at this time to seek in person, the indemnity for the losses of his people, which Sir John — who wished to prevent his absence, at what he considered an important moment, had failed to secure in his own recent visit.

QUEBEC, *Nov.* 9, 1785.
DEAR SIR:

I had the honor to receive your letter of the 6 by express last night at ten o'clock but too late I am sorry to tell you, by two days for producing the effect desired ; Joseph[35] having come to the resolution suddenly of taking passage in the Packet which sailed on Sunday at eleven o'clock in the forenoon ; having been made to believe as he said that the *Madona* was not a safe conveyance from having so few hands, but rather, I am apt to believe from some suspicion that he had entertained of being disappointed in getting away at all if he deferred it till the last Trip, or perhaps artfully wishing to avoid the knowledge of your sentiments which he might expect that the arrival of David at Montreal would produce. In short, my dear Sir John, he was bent upon going and is off notwithstanding my different attempts to dissuade him — offered in such a manner at first as

---

[34] An interesting letter from Col. Guy Johnson to Sir William, too late for insertion here, will be found in Appendix A.
[35] Captain Joseph Brant — Thayendanegea.

not to give him surprize, and at last without disguise of his acting contrary to yours and my wishes and inclinations—all however to no purpose. I have therefore with much regret to return you the letter addressed to Joseph, your other Packet to the Dep. Paymaster General was sent to him.

I congratulate you on the arrival of the Dallis with your things — she got up yesterday but has brought me no Dispatches of any consequence. That we must go on with the Indian business as concerted — keeping them in good humour as much as possible and preaching up patience — & firmness — but by no means encouraging their breaking out. As to anything you may think proper to do to retain those Chiefs & others of influence, or to effect these purposes above mentioned, I shall most readily acquiesce in. With respect to the tools you speak of that were by mistake inserted in the Loyalists Invoice, orders shall be given in consequence of your representation to this effect to deliver up the remainder of them not actually issued for the use of the Indians on your order; as likewise to comply with your requisition for the same purpose to deliver any other articles out of the stores reserved for the use of the Loyalists, being perfectly convinced that from your equal desire to supply and knowledge of the wants of both, that no partial use will ever be made of such discretionary latitude lodged with you.

I return you many thanks and am most flattered by your obliging professions and wishes to myself — request you will make my respects to Lady Johnson and Mrs. Claus, and
  I am Dear Sir with unfeigned regard
   Your very faithful and obedient humble servant
Sir John Johnson, Bart.,   Henry Hope.[36]
 Superintendent General, &c. &c.

Joseph Brant here referred to, is generally recalled by the striking incidents of his life.

A pure blooded Onondaga, the son of a chief, but educated by Sir William's care at Dr. Wheelock's celebrated Moor

---

[36] General Hope was in America in 1775 as Major of the 44th Foot (Gen. Abercrombie's Regt.), and had seen much service there.

school, he proved an apt scholar, soon fitted as an interpreter to Dr. Charles Jeffry Smith, a self sustaining young missionary. Gallantly protecting him when attacked by the Indians, and performing all his duties satisfactorily he won at this period the testimony of Rev. Samuel Kirkland, " he conducted himself so much like a Christian, and a soldier, that he gained great estεem."

Later, he interested himself in the work of the " Society for the Propagation of the Gospel in Foreign parts " and labored with them for the civilization of his people.

When becoming the chief of the Six Nations he wielded a great authority and coöperated with Sir William Johnson, to whom he became allied, as well by affinity as by gratitude. In their close association he doubtless developed the appreciation of the position of his people, and the capacity to vindicate it with an able pen.[37] He visited England in 1775, and again as that letter shows at the end of the war, attracting distinguished attention

---

[37] This letter as to the rights of his people and his own appreciation of honorable dealing is an example.

SIR :   NASSAU, 30 *December*, 1794.

Your letters of the 17th & 20th November, '94, from Konondaigua, I have now before me and have to say, that at all of our meetings during the whole of last summer, our thoughts were solely bent on fixing a boundary line between the confederate Indians and the United States, so as that peace might be established on a solid basis, for which reason we pointed out the line we did, well knowing the justness of it and that it would be ratify'd by the whole Indian confederacy.

As an individual I must regret to find that the Boundary so pointed out has now been abandoned, the establishing of which I am well convinced would have been the means of bringing about a lasting and permanent peace. This object so earnestly to be desired has ever made me exert every nerve, wishing for nothing more than mutual justice. This line you'll recollect was offered to Governor St. Clair at Muskingum, and notwithstanding the two successful campaigns of the Indians after this, I still adhered to the same and still do, this I hope will satisfy you that my wish ever was for Peace, the offer made was rejected by Mr. St Clair, and what the consequences has been you well know, I should be sorry if your efforts were crowned with no better success, as your exertions I hope are not influenced by similar motives with his. You must also recollect that I differed even with my friends respecting this Boundary, and to the two last messages you then received my name was to neither of them, because I thought them too unreasonable, this made me take more pains and trouble to bring the Indians and you to an understanding than I was under any obligation to do — otherwise than humanity dictated to me, having nothing but our mutual interest in view, and as to Politics I study them not, my

partially from his reputation, but also as the chief of the best known tribes of the American Savages, a lion worthy of exhibition. He probably realized then, as he appears to have done, in all the different duties he performed, as their ruler and protector, their inferiority to the white man from the want of that education, which made him sensitive as to their ignorance.

His visit, however, was marked with much appreciation. The King received him, with good humor, even when he refused to kiss his hand, but offered that mark of homage to the Queen. The Duke of Northumberland, Lords Dorchester and Hastings and General Stewart — the son of Bute — who had all served

principle is founded on justice, and justice is all I wish for, and never shall I exert myself on behalf of any nation or nations, let their opinion of me be what it will, unless I plainly see they are just and sincere in their pursuits, doing what in every respect to justice may belong. When I perceive such are the sentiments of a People no endeavors shall be wanting on my part to bring neighbors to a good understanding.

I must again repeat that I am extremely sorry this Boundary so long since pointed out, should have been abandoned, it being an object of such magnitude and which much depends on the whole Indian confederacy being interested. I should therefore have supposed it would have been more for our mutual interest and would have had a better effect, to have dealt upon a larger scale, than within the small compass of the Five Nations, the meeting being intended solely to talk over the business of the Boundary and then to have acquainted the whole confederacy with what had passed, so that something final could have been determined on as all that part of the country is common to the whole. You say on your part everything has been openly and fairly explained and that you shall be disappointed if the Chiefs do not acknowledge your candour, I can for my own part form no opinion, whether it is so or not, being perfectly *ignorant of what has passed, but ever look upon it that business fairly transacted should be adhered to as sacred*. And that you are still ready to make peace with the Western Nations, this has made me say much about the Boundary line, in order that peace and friendship might be established between you, this obliges me to say they ought to have been included in this treaty and to have been consulted with as well as those who were there, they being equally interested with the Six Nations as to this line. *As to the British they are an independent nation, as well as the United States or the Indian Nations and of course act for themselves as all other White nations do.* My mentioning in my letter to you that I was sorry Mr. Johnson was looked upon as a Spy, was because I knew the Five Nations so often erred in their transactions with the White People, it being myself in person from the wish of the Indians that requested Mr. Johnson should go to the Treaty in consequence of which request he was permitted. I was well aware at the same time of the reception he would meet with, as we are an independent People I ever thought our Council should be private, but must at the same time say, we have an unin America, greeted him as a brother veteran and Lords Warwick and Percy, and Dr. Johnson's James Boswell, ordered his portraits, the last, a high testimony that he *was* a " lion."

Yet doubtless he realized his own questionable position, when seeking any trust, with his cultivated nature disguised by the face of a savage. The accompanying letter of Washington displays the general want of confidence in them, by all who were prejudiced against his race.

He adhered to the British Government throughout the war, and after the Treaty of Peace, in which no provision was made as to the territory of his people, struggled to retain what they had formerly possessed. The indefiniteness of the Treaty line,

doubted right to admit at our Councils who we please — of course the United States have it optional whether they will treat or not with any Nation or Nations when Foreign Agents are present.

You seem to think in your letter of the 20th that the Senekas are the Nation most concerned in the Trusts in question agreeable to the lines you point out. At the different Treaties held since the year '83 I allow the Senekas from their proceedings seemed to be the only Nation concerned in that country, although the whole Five Nations have an equal right, one with the other, the country having been obtained by the joint exertions in war with a Powerful Nation formerly living southward of Buffalo Creek called Eries and another Nation then living at Tioga Point, so that by our successes all the country between that and the Mississippi became the joint property of the Five Nations, all other nations now inhabiting this great Tract of Country was allowed to settle by the Five Nations.

This I hope will convince you that the Mohawks have an equal claim and right to receive in proportion with the others of the Five Nations, but as I am ignorant of the Transaction, knowing nothing of what has passed and what was the result of the Treaty, must therefore defer saying anything further on the subject until I know the particulars, which I hope will be ere long. As to the others of the Five Nations residing on the Grand River they must answer for themselves. I am not so particular in this as I might be, seeing no great necessity for it, as I hope to see General Chapin ere long. In reading the Speech you have sent me I perceive that you say we requested you might be sent to Kindle the Council Fire &c. This I know to be a mistake, in our speech to General Chapin we wished the President of the United States to send a Commissioner to our Fire Place at Buffaloe Creek (your name being mentioned). Not that you was to come and kindle a Council Fire elsewhere — & that you requested our assistance to bring about a Peace, &c. — You did and everything has been done by us faithfully and sincerely by pointing out the Medicine that would accomplish it, your relinquishing parts of your claims in the Indian Country. *You also say I told Genl Chapin at Winnys that it was the British that prevented the Treaty taking place. I said so then and still do. What enabled me to say so was the Gentlemen belonging to the Indian Department in that quarter interfering in the business.*

which long remained as flexible as a wire fence, moved back and forth at will, even looking for the sources of the Mississippi at the Lake of the Woods, instead of Itaska lake, far below, and which required four subsequent treaties, an arbitration, and a war, to settle ; seems a reasonable cause for discussions, attempts at treaties, and long complications.

These letters to Colonels Pickering and Monroe are merely suggestions of the many records existing of his capacity and persistency, in seeking to protect and retain what his forefathers had held by an undisputed title, before even the Johnsons had come with the authority of conquest, to divide it.

When Gist, the companion of Washington, was exploring the valley of the Ohio, in 1752, a Delaware chief demanded of him:

Had the line as pointed out by us been accepted by the United States their interference would not have prevented Peace then taking place as the Five Nations had pledged themselves to see it ratified. As to the business of the White Nations I perceive it at present to be a lottery which will be uppermost cannot be known until drawn, the most powerful no doubt will succeed, but let who will he successful our situation is the same, as we still have whites to deal with whose aims are generally similar. You mention the People of France took the Indian method. All their warriors turned out. The Indian warriors are always ready to turn out to defend their just rights. But Indian warriors would not be ready to Butcher in an inhuman shocking manner their King, Queen, Nobles and others, this is acting worse than what is called Savage. The Indians are not entirely destitute of humanity, but from every appearance it has fled from France. I must therefore say the French have not acted as the Indians do. You likewise mention that you told the Deputies from the Westward who met you at this place, that though you was willing to run a new line yet it was impossible to make the Ohio the Boundary, this I believe is a mistake as the word Ohio was never mentioned at that time. You may rest assured that I do not swerve from any expressions I have made use of. I know the necessity for being candid, especially at this critical juncture. I still earnestly hope that Peace may be established without further bloodshed & that Friendship may reign between the People of the United States and the Indian Nations, this be assured is the Sincere wish of

         Sir, Your Most Obedient
           Humble Servant
Timothy Pickering, Esqr.   Jos. Brant.

Col. Pickering had been employed for some years in these negotiations as being a member of the President's Cabinet as Post Master General and in this year made Secretary of War. Another very interesting and able letter of Brant to Colonel James Monroe in four neatly written pages is omitted, as partially printed in the 2d Vol. of his Life.

"Where *are* the lands of the Indians? the French claim all on one side of the river, and the English all on the other."³⁸ Such was the position of the heritage which Brant believing that he was born to maintain and transmit, was then losing.

Failing, as many have done before and since, he retired into Canada and spent his later years under the protection of those with whom he had made common cause, but personally so delicately accepting their bounty, as in one instance to question his own right to a pension, as a retired military officer.

Thomas Campbell, lived to correct — in a foot note — his record of Brant's cruelty, in his widely read "Gertrude of Wyoming," but its subject who had grieved over it, had died too soon for the comforting retraction. His absence on that occasion, threw the weight of the massacre on a white savage, Colonel John Butler, who doubtless had the same authority as that conferred on his kinsman and subordinate by the commission annexed.³⁹

Brant was, however, present at the battle of Minisink, where great cruelty was displayed, for which he has been censured. If he was responsible for it, it detracts from many other evidences of his humanity in warfare, and shows the trace of the savage element in his character, when fired by war.

³⁸ Griswold and Lossing's Washington.

³⁹ This commission indicating care in its instructions, now unusual in such documents, and wear from use. is that of Walter Butler, noted both for his efficiency and cruelty, killed at Canada Creek, on the 29th of October, 1781, by a force under Col. Marinus Willett, while retreating from a raid to Warren's Bush, and his former home, in the year succeeding the expedition of Sir John.

GUY CARLETON, Knight of the Bath, Captain General and Governor in Chief of the province of Quebec and Territories depending thereon, &c., &c., General and Commander in-Chief of his Majesty's Forces in said Province and the Frontiers thereof &c., &c. To WALTER BUTLER, Esq., Greeting:

Reposing special trust and Confidence, in your Loyalty, Courage and good Conduct, I do by these Presents Constitute and appoint you to be *Captain in a Corps of Rangers*

He would appear to have been a man of large capacity; and his record a noticeable evidence of the result of its development in time of peace, by the same wise appliances, now interesting to examine in use, at the school at Hampton, Va., in charge of General Armstrong, and probably at the two others, at Forest Grove for the western, and Carlisle for the eastern section. Such efforts, are in accordance with the dying suggestions of Brant to his nephew, "Have pity on the poor Indians; if you can get any influence with the great, endeavor to do them all the good you can."

His life by Colonel Stone, a work of singular interest, gives full detail of his career, in part early collected in his old neighborhood—a fine edition of it printed by the late Joel Munsell, of Albany, largely with his own hand, assists to cause the latter to be recalled by some collectors, as the Albany "Caxton."

It is just to record a dissenting opinion as to the proper treatment of the remaining Aborigines. It differs from those of Colonel Brisbane, and other regular officers who have served amongst them, and of some who have visited the border posts and studied the effect of the contact of races. Captain Payne

to serve with the Indians during the Rebellion. Whereof *John Butler*, *Esq.*, is *Major Commandant.* You are therefore carefully and diligently to discharge the duty of captain by exercising and well disciplining both the Inferior Officers and Soldiers of that Corps, and I do hereby command them to obey you as their Captain, and you are to observe and follow such Orders and directions as you shall from Time to Time receive from me, your Major Commandant, or any other Superior Officer, according to the rules and discipline of War. In pursuance of the trust hereby reposed in you. *Given* under my hand and Seal at Arms, at *Quebec*, this twentieth day of December, 1777, and in the Eighteenth year of the Reign of our Sovereign Lord, *George the Third*, by the Grace of God, of Great Britain, France and Ireland, King, Defender of the Faith, and so forth, GUY CARLETON.
By His Excellency's Command, FRANCIS LE MAISTRE.
Walter Butler, Esq., Captain of a Corps of Rangers, to serve with the Indians during the Rebellion.

recently arrested by our troops when raiding in the Indian Territory, and affecting to be a humane man in his way, says:

"Tell the Herald, that the policy of myself and followers is not to resist the government, so we came along with the troops when we were told to come. * * * * "There is a class of people who are eternally howling that they are afraid the white man may crowd the Indian. They are the people who sit in their houses, cut their coupons and read gush about the poor Indian. They don't want farms and a living, they have already got them and have no sympathy for those who are poor and want homes. They would rather see the poor man starve, than to have their picture of the noble redman chasing the wild gazelle over an eternal meadow with a babbling brook, destroyed."

The writer must be aware that while the area of the Indian Territory is less than 69,000 square miles, that of Texas is 274,356, large enough it would appear, for the accommodation of the rights of the settler, and the native. That there is a vast area of land in the west and south-west, already open "to those who want farms." If any person desires to trace the origin and progress of such methods as he proposes, for securing the territory of the "noble red man," without consideration or equivalent, he can find them successively detailed in this "Life of Brant," and many other works referring to the same period. If such acquisitions are still indispensible to the progress of civilization, might we not devise a way of acquiring the territory consistent with its teachings, which would be more creditable in future history than that of involving constant collision and shedding of blood.

Lord Sydney simply recognizes Johnson's official position, in fixing a temporary salary, which even with the difference in the value of money, would be a moderate compensation now for a subordinate civil officer.

WHITEHALL, 20 *August*, 1785.

SIR :

I am sorry that it is not in my power before your departure for Quebec, to acquaint you that some decision had taken place with respect to your salary as Superintendent of Indian Affairs. I hope that it will very shortly be fixed, in the meantime I am authorized to inform you that you may draw upon the Commander-in-chief in Canada, for the usual salary of One Thousand pounds per annum, until you receive further direction from me. I flatter myself that I shall be able to write to you fully upon this subject by the next Packet that sails for Quebec, and you may be assured that no endeavour of mine will be wanting to obtain the augmentation of your salary which you desire, and place it upon a permanent footing, I have the honor to be, with regard,

Sir, Your Most Obedient
Humble Servant,
SYDNEY.[40]

Sir John Johnson, Bart.

No British officer in service in the Revolution, would appear to have left America with more reciprocal hostile feeling than General Gage, the earliest commander of the King's Troops in that war. The certificate of his son has no interest, beyond a reference to his father's habit of business.

[40] Hon. Thomas Townshend who on the dissolution of Lord North's ministry had become Lord Sydney.

GENERAL GAGE'S CERTIFICATE TO SIR JOHN'S DEPUTY.

I certify that Colonel Guy Johnson took an active part in favour of the British Government from the first appearance of a Revolt in North America, that he did his duty as became a faithful Subject in his Department of Superintendent of Indian Nations and kept those Tribes in his Majestys Interest and defeated the Endeavors of the Rebels to alienate their affections from the King, and to induce them to appear in Arms against his Government. That he assembled a large Body of Indians and joined General Carlton in Canada.

THOS GAGE.

Given under my hand this 21st day of June 1785.

MR. CHEW[41] attorney for Sir John Johnson having applied to me for copies of the accounts which Sir Wm. Johnson Super Intendent for Indian Affairs transmitted to my father General Gage deceased during his Commanding His Majestys Troops in America, and for copies of the Warrants he gave for the Payment thereof, I can only say that my fathers papers have not come immediately under my inspection or can I say positively whether the copies of those Accounts and Warrants are with them, but am certain that it was a Rule with him to see accounts made clear and plain and when he gave Warrants for the Payment the Warrants were annexed to the Accounts and transmitted by him to the Pay Office in London where they now no doubt may be found.

H. GAGE.[42]

Old Aboresford Nov. 16, 1787.
To Mr. Chew, Attorney to Sir John Johnson.

[41] Captain Joseph Chew, a prisoner to the French when commanding a detachment reconnoitering 19 June, 1747. A legatee of 250 acres in Sir William Johnson's will, as his "much esteemed friend and old acquaintance" and father of his god son. Also one of the executors.

[42] Henry Viscount Gage, retired Major of the 93 Regt. of Foot, a grandson of Peter Kemble of the Kings Council of New Jersey, also the ancestor of the late well esteemed Gouverneur Kemble, of New York.

Three of these jetsams of Time, suggest the continued expense which Great Britain was incurring in the charge of her Indian population even in time of peace, and whether it was in consideration of their former service in war.

Guy, Lord Dorchester General and Commander-in-chief of his Majesty's Forces in North America.

To Thomas Boone, Deputy Paymaster General, etc., Warrant to pay Sir John Johnson, etc., etc., Nine Thousand pounds sterling in dollars at 4s. 8d., each, for services of " persons employed and sundry disbursements of the Department of Indian Affairs under his Superintendency between 25th Dec., 1786, and 24th March, 1787."

Quebec, 9th November, 1786.

DORCHESTER.

To the Right Honorable Guy, Lord Dorchester, Capt General and Governor-in-Chief of the Colonies of Quebec, Nova Scotia, New Brunswick & their Dependencies, Vice Admiral of the same General and Commander-in-Chief of all His Majestys Forces in Said Colonies & in the Island of Newfoundland &c &c.

The Memorial of Sir John Johnson Baronet Superintendent General & Inspector General of Indian Affairs.

Humbly Sheweth. That your Memorialist is in want of £4319 5s. 8d. sterling to enable him to pay Persons employed in the Department of Indian Affairs under his Superintendency between the 25 December 1786 and 24 December 1787 as per abstract annexed. We therefore pray your Excellencys Warrant on the Deputy Paymaster General for the above sum.

JOHN JOHNSON.

QUEBEC 16 *April*, 1788.

ANOTHER ORDER by Lord Dorchester, in favor of Sir John as Superintendent and Inspector General of Indian Affairs, for Two Thousand pounds, for incidental expenses, between 25th December, 1786, and 24th December, 1787.

in the Revolution. 71

Both signed by Dorchester and Captain Francis Le Maistre, the Governor's A. D. C. and Secretary and endorsed by Sir John Johnson.

This doubtless to be used in a claim for indemnity, refers to a useful officer of the British Government in Canada during the Revolution.

In the Exchequer In the matter of Sir John Johnson, Baronet, the legal personal representative of Sir William Johnson, Baronet, his late Father, deceased, late Superintendent of Indian Affairs in North America.

[STAMP]

Thomas Wallis, late Assistant in the office of the Secretary to the Commander-in-Chief in North America, now of Hertford street, Mayfair, in the County of Middlesex, Gentleman, maketh oath and saith, that he has known General Sir Frederick Haldimand for fourteen years and that the words and figures "London the 14th of August, 1787," and the name "Fred Haldimand" appearing to be written and subscribed at the foot of the account and certificate marked with the letter X now produced, are the proper handwriting of the said General Sir Fred Haldimand,[43] and were written and subscribed by him in the presence of this deponent, and the said General Sir Fred Haldimand after he had so subscribed the same, delivered the said produced account and certificate to this deponent, and directed him to deliver the same to Mr. Chew, attorney to the said Sir William Johnson.   THOS. WALLIS.

Sworn at my house in St. John street }
the 11th April, 1788, before me. }
                            J. A. EYRE.

Sir John here appears in a civil office usually awarded in British Colonies, as a mark of especial consideration.

---

[43] Born and died at Switzerland, at first in Prussian service, but entered the English with Col. Bouquet. Came to America as Lt. Col. 60 Royal American Regt. in 1757; distinguished at Ticonderoga in 1750; defended Oswego in 1759; with Amherst at Montreal in 1760; as Colonel at Pensacola 1767; home informing ministry as to Colonies in 1775; b ick as Lieut. General in 1776; succeeded Carleton as Gov. of Canada in 1778 and until 1784; died in 1791.

QUEBEC, 1 *May*, 1787..

RECEIVED from Henry Caldwell, Esq., Acting Receiver General of the Province of Quebec the sum of Fifty Pounds Sterling, being for my Salary as a Member of the Legislative Council of the Province, from 1st November, 1786, to 30 April, 1787, pursuant to his Excellency, Governor Lord Dorchester's warrant dated 1st May 1787, for which I have signed Two Receipts of this Tenor and Date.
£50 Sterling.   JOHN JOHNSON.

Apparently a moderate compensation compared with that of later law-makers, and especially well earned if the *quality* of legislation was equivalent to its *quantity*. In this it would markedly differ from much that has been *condensed* into portly volumes as the brain food offered by the deliberative wisdom of other bodies when sitting for a similar period. Perhaps he divined how much easier it is to enact, than in all cases to comprehend. How doubtful the *intention* of the law maker often proves to others, and how much special legislation is rendered unnecessary by general acts, if sought for. He doubtless discovered, as many legislators have, that there were more debaters than listeners, more movers than seconders, and that it is easier to criticise than to originate.

The remaining letter borrowed from a friend's exhaustive collection of Americana merely displays neighborly kindness to one who sympathised in sentiment and destiny, by taking refuge from imprisonment for political offences in Canada with the writer.

DR SIR   JOHNSONS HALL 25 *July* 1775.

The bearer will deliver you some provisions & clothes and Mr Clement will give you a paper containing a Ten pound note which I received from Mrs White this morning. The Indians having desired some cash from me to expend when they come

amongst the inhabitants in Canada, which I have not to give them I must beg you will supply them & charge it to Colonel Johnson. If you have forgot anything and I can be of service to you I beg you'll mention it. God bless you.
To Alexander White Esq.   Yrs   J. Johnson.[44]

These random notes as to the Johnsons suggest reflections as to the quality of loyalty, even in an adversary, to one whose sympathies, studies and collections, have for years been devoted to appreciative illustration of the achievements of their opponents and a jealous watchfulness to their use. Although sketched from a different standpoint, he trusts that his conclusions will accord with those which a friend is preparing under different inspirations, at a point too remote for comparison. The absence of Memoirs, Diaries,[45] and even of comprehensive letters on these details is to be regretted.

[44] *This* and one other letter belonging to Dr. Thomas Addis Emmett, all of the other letters and papers in that of the contributor. As to Sheriff White and the circumstances under which it was written, vide Stone's "Life of Brant," Vol. I, pp. 101-6-7-12, 364.

[45] There appears to be a resemblance — probably often noticed by others, between the useful oyster fisher, who delves with his rake into the muddy bottom, for the bivalve and the less widely appreciated labor of one who dives for costly pearls in the turbid waters of forgotten fact.

Many amateur Collectors of fragmentary history are scattered over the country purchasing and articulating disjointed material, and quietly working with the devotion voluntarily displayed by Old Mortality in *his* specialty of restoring the dilapidated tombstones of people he had never seen. No writer on American History has elucidated more epitaphs of the humbler patriots, than Dr. Lossing, whose "Field Books" are in effect, Biographical Lexicons.

Another instance of a renaissance of valuable historical waifs, germain to the name of Burgoyne, elsewhere referred to, as connected with one associated with his career once as his fellow soldier, then his conqueror, and styled by him his "Accoucheur!" A large portion of the military papers, and order books, of General Gates, after slumbering in his muniment box for over threescore years, had recently a new birth, in falling into the remarkable Emmet Collection.

A part of them through the active enterprise of Mr. John Austin Stevens, were used to add value of the word "Resurgam" by their publication in the October, 1880 — Gates — number of the "Magazine of American History." They arise to dispel many errors, disseminated in American History. They show, that after his probably ill-advised advance at Camden, when driven from a remote part of the field by the precipitate flight of the North Carolina militia — con-

Without these evidences, many, intending to leave an honorable record, will always go down to posterity as responsible from their position, in political or military life, for action of their associates, which they personally abhorred, perhaps opposed, in its progress, or at worst finally submitted to, from fear of retaliation, on some proper object.

Samuel Pepys, who recorded in his Diary with the experiences of an unimportant life, much random fact, some of which subsequently become of historical interest, is now being recalled — two centuries later — by the erection of a Memorial in London, in the place where he worshipped and rests. It would have been interesting if Johnson himself, or some Pepysian annotator of events, sharing his confidence and his tent or home, had jotted down the circumstances attending his arrest, parole,

---

fronted by well drilled regulars — ignorant by this separation, of the stand de Kalb was making, with the gallant Maryland and Delaware line and a few militia, having the benefit of their near example, that he, with General Caswell and other officers, struggled for many miles to rally them, so "flying" with them before the pursuing enemy, in an effort to bring them back. That instead of his "hair growing grey as he fled," in his letter to the President of Congress, Hillsborough, 20th August, 1780, he says, " By this time the militia had taken to the woods in all directions, and I concluded with General Caswell, to retire towards Charlotte, I got there late in the night — but reflecting that there was neither arms, ammunition, nor any prospect of collecting any Force at that Place, adequate to the defence of the Country — I proceeded with all possible despatch hither; to endeavour to fall upon some plan, in conjunction with the Legislature of this State, for the defence of so much thereof as it is yet possible, to save from the enemy." Whatever the error in his strategy may have been — and it is always easier to criticize than to plan, his course from his arrival seems by many letters energetic, and that of one intent on developing order out of chaos. While mortified with the condition into which he had fallen, he does not appear to have lost heart or hope, and continued his exertions apparently conscious that his prestige as a soldier was lost, until he was superceded by General Greene, who reaped a harvest of laurels on the ground on which his own crop had been blighted.

A recently printed sketch of Colonel Anthony Walton White — who commanded, with Col. Lee, detachments of Continental Cavalry lying near, and only waiting for their horses to have filled a special want at Camden, and whose equipment appears to have been a cause of special anxiety to General Gates — published with a fine military portrait by Sharples, and prepared under the direction of his grandson, Mr. Evans, is another interesting renaissance.

and its claimed infringement or whether he considered it violated and withdrawn by the attempted arrest; and also if at Klocks Farm he left the field unwounded, deserting a command with which he evidently displayed marked courage, in the contest of the day. As to the facts connected with the parole, careful consideration even in the absence of such evidence, would doubtless now convince any fair opponent, that the judgment of some history has been biased, by the then obnoxious position of the actor.

It was exacted, by a display of force, from one who although holding a Major General's commission, had committed no overt act of hostility against the *de facto* government, existing when he was arrested by the order of the " Provincial Congress " of the State, and the " Albany Committee " bodies,

In the field of early southern history there is probably no amateur — amongst the many who are quietly interested in similar labor — who has more liberally contributed valuable privately printed facts than Colonel Charles C. Jones, Jr., of Augusta. His "Siege of Savannah in 1779," and another of that of 1864, are amongst his valuable works. While the humane administration of General Ogelthorpe, the remarkable character who founded Georgia, has been largely recalled by his pen; his " Historical Sketches of Tomo-chi-chi, the Mico of the Yamacraws "— an important factor in American History in his period, but whose name now would require a special introduction even to many general readers — affords testimony, based on information, of the merit of another Aboriginal ruler.

The correspondence of General Daniel Morgan, the hero of Cowpens, including much of Washington, and Lafayette especially his friend, having fallen into the writer's collection, in a manner very satisfactory to his family, an opportunity was soon availed of to use it in recalling his usefulness. Happening to receive an invitation from Mayor Courtenay—a zealous appreciator and collector of Charleston Historical Relics which he liberally restores to their appropriate form and place—and a committee of officers and citizens to be present at the centennial celebration of that battle, the key to Yorktown, it appeared that he would be best represented, by contributing copies of all of the official papers connected with that event. They were recognized, as an articulate apparition of the many writers amidst the scenes of their former action, by the posterity of many of them ; filled much of the "Charleston News" of the day, with *local*, if old, intelligence, and have taken one hundred new chances of preservation in a privately printed brochure, neatly prepared by Captain Dawson one of its editors, who sympathizes in the past, while active in his present. These are referred to here, merely as instances of the value of the preservation, and the recurrence of appropriate opportunity to perform an easy duty.

created by an uprising of an indignant people, and *six months after* that incident occurred, formed by the Declaration of Independence into part of a nation *de jure*.

If it had been executed after that period, doubtless the sense of obligation would have been stronger upon a soldier, but at the time the authority of Great Britain controlled a large portion of the Colonies — restive under its restraint — and its local authorities were in power at New York, as in Canada, still recognized as the only lawful rulers by a large portion of the people.

To a person representing large interests, and the head of a family, this interregnum must have been a period for anxiety, and adhering to the old government, made him a subject for suspicion and dislike, to those who had so aggregated for the assertion of grievances, still hoping for concessions to justify their dissolution, but preparing if necessary, in the impending struggle to establish their permanency. To this administration of public affairs, not yet made permanent by the action of Congress on the 4th of the ensuing July, he had refused to give his adhesion, to sign the articles of association, or to recognize its authority, declaring that he would "rather that his head should be cut off," than unite in a conflict with his native government, the authority of which he doubtless hoped would be soon reasserted. In this, he became an obstacle to the popular movement, and was from his influence and authority, a subject for supression or control. His every movement was watched and discussed, and it was claimed that he was fortifying his house, organizing his retainers, and co-operating with the Indians for resistance, yet there is no clear evidence that he pursued any course unusual to his position as a citizen and a magistrate, in troubled times.

But his presence was esteemed a danger in itself and his removal a necessity which knew no law. General Schuyler arrested him, with a large, unresisted military force, in January, 1776; he was sent to Fishkill and submitted to a parole, not to bear arms against the *de facto* authority which exacted it, or to leave the vicinity of his home. It is probable that he sought in this an opportunity to arrange his affairs, until either concession or suppression restored the authority of his government. For some causes, probably the continued suspicion of danger from his private communications, his capture and confinement, which would have naturally terminated his protection and the mutuality of his parole was decided upon, and Colonel Dayton stopped at the Hall, on his way to Canada, to make his arrest, but found that Johnson, advised of his coming, had escaped into Canada, the nearest accessible stronghold of the authority he recognized. His endurance of nineteen days of terrible suffering in this, his winter journey through the Adirondacks, attested his physical courage; and the leaving all he valued behind him, subordinate to a sense of duty, his remarkable loyalty. The romantic incidents attending Lady Johnson's share in her husband's downfall, will doubtless be appropriately given by her kinsman. He cannot fail to show, that her married life justified the promise which Colonel Guy Johnson discerned before that event, when meeting her while in New York as described in the accompanying letter. (Appendix A.)

Such a parole enforced on a citizen by an as yet temporarily constituted and semi-representative body, and the knowledge

that it was to be substituted by imprisonment, from precaution
and not for crime, would appear to differ materially from one
exacted after conquest in the field, and that its essence was
in the application of Major Dugald Dalgetty's maxim, "*fides
et fiducia relativa sunt.*"

Many expert military critics have considered the question of
the obligations of paroles, with varied latitude. Some have pronounced this one no longer obligatory on a prisoner, who was
aware of its intended breach by the giver, and that the law of
nature overrode the dictates of a nice sense of honor — best
appreciated in another — and an escape after warning of the
intention of the withdrawal of protection was as justifiable
before, as after its execution.

But there is a precedent apparently applicable, which illustrates the difference of sympathy from surroundings, and how
the same claimed offence is viewed by the friends or enemies
of the actor. Those who have remembered the blame which
has attached to Sir John, should examine the different sentiments
called forth for one who suffered for what he alone was censured.
This parallel case, was that of Colonel Isaac Hayne,* a prominent patriot in South Carolina. He had served in the defence
of Charleston, with the cavalry operating outside of the city,
but not included in the capitulation. Afterwards he considered
that the protection of his family residing on the Edisto, required
that he should accept a parole from the captors, only obtained,
by signing with a protest as to service, the oath of allegiance,
prescribed by Sir Henry Clinton's proclamations.

This exposed him to the annoyance of frequent calls *for* his
service as a soldier, due by that obligation to the King, and
when Gen. Greene advanced in 1781, *considering* the British

* See Ramsey's Revolution in S. C., Vol. II, p. 277, etc.

control ended, he again took the field, was captured, tried, and executed, by Lord Rawdon, at the instigation of Col. Nesbit Balfour, the commandant, recalled there still as a tyrant. The whole country was filled with denunciation of this cruelty. The Duke of Richmond censured it in Parliament and Balfour was rendered notable for his unfeeling disregard to the appeal of his family and friends for mercy, while the name of Hayne is remembered, by collectors of American History, as a martyr to a popular and successful cause. Had Sir John been captured in either of his bold invasions, made additionally perilous by that impending charge, he might have suffered, even by the influence of his exasperated neighbors, from whom he had parted with mutual antipathy. His daring on such other occasions, discredits the tradition of his flight, unwounded, in advance of his command, at Klocks Field, and makes it seem an instance of misrepresentation unanswered, and accepted by credulous History as the gift of irresponsible tradition.

It is notable that the "Annals of Tryon County," which William W. Campbell, an estimable gentleman and painstaking collector, residing at Cherry Valley, prepared many years ago,* in connection with a society formed at that place for the collection of Local History, in describing the battle, and alluding to the bravery of Johnson's troops, omits this sudden departure which must have reached him there in rumor, rejected as fact.

The tradition of his flight from Klocks Field without referring to his disabled condition, perhaps arose with exasperated neighbors while suffering from his undoubtedly vindictive ravages, whose patriotism was naturally stimulated by the possession of his abandoned property, and from whom any sympathy would be as unnatural as that of the huntsman for a

* Border Warfare of New York and Annals, etc., 1849.

wounded, stag, which had ceased to stand at bay. That his accepted government appreciated the audacity of his three incursions, and subsequently repeatedly honored him with commands and places of trust, proves at least their continued confidence in his courage and honor. That any of these questions should remain open for discussion, more than a century afterwards sustains the views elsewhere expressed, of the untold value of impartial and carefully prepared cotemporary history.

In any event he had opportunity to regret in a long life of exile, the beautiful home which he had lost by the rigor with which his native State adhered to its rule of confiscation. He resided afterwards in Canada, and is still represented by many distinguished descendants. When he died he afforded to posterity an opportunity to consider that best test for judgment of the action of another " put yourself in his place."

Although prompted by a sense of the justice of availing of the opportunity to say a word in defence of those whose records have left their names unpopular, the writer is satisfied that their vindication has been delayed too long to influence some whose opinions are hereditary, and have never been modified by the softening effects of research.[46]

One who has given his attention to historical collections, and has completed series of the letters of the Signers, the Generals, and the prominent actors of the Colonial and Revolutionary periods, has naturally sought for information as to their inner, as well as their printed lives, and incidentally as to

---

[46] It appears proper to say that these sentiments, — not influenced by any personal considerations, — are somewhat contrary to the writer's earlier and more crude convictions, derived from antecedents, in that period, and from the early settlement of New York, identified with the popular cause, and often then and since by succession, under the union of the States, aiding — sometimes effectively — in its civil service, and in every war.

those of their cotemporaries, and of the circumstances which governed all of them.

This naturally inspires a comparison with the more familiar ones of their successors, and of their relative administration of public trust. It may even induce a conjecture as to the result — if it were possible to make the experiment — of placing the members of the Congress of 1776, in the seats of a few of its recent representatives. The alternative, by a substitution of many of our present for those past law-makers, would give occupation for a stronger imagination, in realizing the uses of the modern appliances of legislation in those time-honored chairs.

Were such transpositions of men of the present for those of that important crisis possible, might it not be less difficult, even after a century of brilliant national prosperity, affording opportunities to individuals which few then enjoyed, and a condensation of events which no other nation has probably ever witnessed in a similar period, to select a substitute for Sir John Johnson, were he all that vague tradition and prejudice has pictured him to be, using every appliance that he is said to have resorted to in seeking to claim an inheritance of which he felt himself unjustly deprived, than to discover a second Washington, deferring compensation, neglecting, in his negation of self, his own ample estate, to battle to secure the property of others, subjecting himself to the jealousy of those who coveted his honors, but not the cares and exposure[47] which earned them,

---

[47] To His Excellency, George Washington, Esq., General, &c.,
Sir:
Whereas, David Matthews, Esq., stands charged with dangerous Designs and treasonable Conspiracies against the Rights and Liberties of the United Colonies of America. We do, in Pursuance of a certain Resolve of Congress of this Colony of the twentieth day of June, instant, authorize and request you to cause the said David Matthews to be with all his papers forthwith apprehended and secured, and

devoting his manhood to his country, and finally epitomising his life, as an example to the temporarily refractory troops at Newburg, by saying — when compelled to resort to his glasses in deciphering his conclusive appeal to their patriotism and endurance — "You see gentlemen, that I have not only grown gray, but blind, in your service."

To write the name of Washington is a temptation to the digression of an American pen, even when proposing to speak more specially of those whom he conquered, and only incident. ally of the victors.

Collectors of unprinted Historical Material — often classed as Autographs — were long accustomed to attach some importance, in discerning the character and surroundings of the writer, both to his manner of expression, and his chirography. This theory has been sustained by many able authorities, including Dr. Joseph G. Cogswell, formerly of the Astor Library.

that returns be made to us of the manner in which this Warrant shall be executed in order that the same may be made known to the said Congress.
Given under our hands this twenty-first day of June, 1776. PHILIP LIVINGSTON,
JOHN JAY,
GOV. MORRIS.

General Greene is desired to have the within Warrant executed with precision and exactness, by one o'clock the ensuing morning, by a careful officer.
FRIDAY AFTERNOON, *June* 20, 1776.   G. WASHINGTON.

LONG ISLAND, *June* 22d, 1776.
In obedience to the within Order and Warrant, I sent a Detachment of my Brigade under the Command of Col. Vernon, to the house of the within named David Matthews, Esq., at Flat Bush, who surrounded his house and seized his person precisely at the hour of one this morning. After having made him a Prisoner, diligent search was made after his Papers but none could be found, notwithstanding great care was taken that none of the Family should have the least opportunity to remove or destroy them.   NATHANIEL GREENE.

THIS PAPER, if earlier discovered, should have been appropriate additional material for "Minutes of the Trial and Examination of Certain Persons in the Province of New York, charged with being Engaged in a Conspiracy against the Authority of the Congress and the Liberties of America." Printed in London, by I. Bew, in 1786, and reprinted in an edition of one hundred copies, entitled "Minutes of Conspiracy against the Liberties of America," by John Campbell, in Philadelphia, 1865, describing the details of "the Hickey Plot" for the poisoning of Washington,

Any even fancied value in this belief, is becoming obsolete as applicable to later correspondence, in an unprecedented progress, crowding the events of life, and increasing the value of the hour. Rapidity of thought and action, now conveyed upon paper involves brevity, curtails compliment, and disregards form.

In the day when magazines were scarcely known, newspapers were small and rare, devoted principally to advertisements, with current events condensed, and even discussion by tracts occasional; a letter, as a comprehensive means of communication, was an important channel of intelligence. Its dignified foolscap, or "letter size;" emblazoned with water line, and adorned by a gilt edge, was covered by a carefully selected "quill," with at least three pages of public or private

by that man, one of his Life Guards, who was executed. Governor Tryon, who was quartered on the Duchess of Gordon, a vessel lying in the harbor — and singularly named after the lady whom Gen. Staats Long Morris, the loyalist member of a patriot family, married — was supposed to be the instigator; the medium was David Matthews, the Mayor, who admitted supplying money at least, for arms, and who was sentenced to death, but reprieved and sent to Connecticut, from whence he escaped; the method to poison Washington with green peas which were provided, and on being tested on some poultry, proved fatal; and the result to be a rising in arms, in case of success. It was detected by the disclosure made through his housekeeper, the daughter of Samuel Frances, the innkeeper at the corner of Broad and Pearl, where Washington afterwards bid adieu to his officers. The seat of the conspiracy, was Cortie tavern, between "Richmond Hill," "Bayard's Woods," and "Lispenard's meadow," near the now intersection of Spring and Wooster streets. This order of arrest was issued on the next day, only three days before Lord Howe's arrival, soon followed by the Battle of Long Island, the retreat of Washington, and the British occupation of the city, attended by the confusion in which, Matthews probably escaped. A trifling circumstance, the careful erasing of a word with a penknife, over which the word "within," is written in Washington's endorsement, displays the coolness and method in writing referred to, even at a moment when his life was beset by assassins. The other papers above alluded to as printed, were those of the Secretary of the Committee of Congress signing this order for arrest. The accompanying letter is from Richard Cumberland, the well known essayist and author of many plays and brochures, a retired Secretary of the Board of Trade, and apparently, from the contents of a number of letters from which it is selected, an attachè and purveyor of Lord George Germain, State Secretary, is addressed to William Woodfall, before the public at this period, and prosecuted by the Crown as the publisher of the "Letters

intelligence, conveyed in well formed characters, with dignified assurances of consideration and respect. It was generally closed with wax, and impressed with the seal, which then dangled from the writer's "fob," all in such form as to make it presentable to a friend, or to a neighborhood, according to its privacy or public import. Then conveyed in a "mastship" or packet, in a lumbering "stage-wagon," or by a private express, its receipt was a sensation, and it was generally preserved as an object of value, often to arise years afterwards, permanent from its solid material, and perhaps to find new appreciation in a historical collection, to solve a doubt, or suggest an inquiry.

Rare papers like rare paintings still command competition, showing continued appreciation. (Appendix E.)

Such was the "golden age" of the collectors only recently terminated by the Telegraph, where each *word* has a cost as well as a value; the Postal Card, commanding condensation and

of Junius." He has an equally surviving recollection, as associated with the original Mr. Walter, of the *London Times*, in experiments in printing by steam.

SIR: DRAYTON, *Tuesday Morning*,

Since I wrote to you and enclosed ye *Boston Gazette*, a messenger is arrived with ye news of ye reduction of forts Washington and Lee, and with despatches from ye General, which I make do doubt occasioned the publishing of an Extra Gazette last night. This intelligence would have been brought us to town directly, if Lord George had not been indisposed with a cold and swelled face, so that we shall not be in town till Friday morning. Anything in my power to communicate to you shall readily be done, and I am very sorry that my distance makes it not practicable by this opportunity. Ye loyal Mayor of New York has made his escape from Litchfield and returned to that City. He reports the situation of the people in Connecticut to be that of men heartily weary of their cause and its conductors. That the hospitals are miserably attended and served, where great numbers are lost for want of common care. That there are small, or no hopes, of another Army being raised, the eyes of the common people being generally open to their situation. That a sovereign contempt for their officers prevails universally, that they say Lee (Gen. Charles) will not engage for fear of being taken and hanged and that ye fame and popularity of Gen. Washington is greatly gone down.

Many particulars may occur worthy the public notice when I return to town and get my letters, &c. I am, Sir,

Your Most Obedient Ser'vt,

Mr. William Woodfall. R. CUMBERLAND.

in the Revolution. 85

disclaiming privacy, and the Monograph, with such Napoleonic terseness and brief detail as is necessary to intelligibility with little regard to form. These last appliances tended in our recent war, to condense such full narratives of action as had been usual in the past, leaving it to the comprehensive and indispensable newspapers, published in keeping with the progress of the age, and to their correspondents to form the public sentiment of its course and results as they appeared to them. It remains for the government to perfect its history, by instituting a careful analysis of such narrative, and by the use of the public records, the last of which is believed to be now in progress, and if so will correct many errors, known to have often unavoidably crept into more hastily prepared impressions.

At the period now referred to, such notable persons in its history as Washington, Sir Henry Clinton, Greene, Cornwallis, and Gates — when dispensing with the services of aid or secretary — and, in fact, all educated persons, from sovereign to citizen, found time to convey their thoughts in letters thus carefully expressed and gracefully executed, as though to combine in both contents and form, a courtesy to the person addressed, and to suggest if not to prove, that the writer was, as a "gentleman of the old school," at least "to all polite." Perhaps, letters of this period which are preserved, commend in their *ensemble* this style, which is necessarily passing away from the causes referred to.

At least it recalls its recollection with respect, to say that it everywhere characterizes the manner of communicating the plainest sentiments by Washington! The large number of his letters, still carefully preserved, show his industry; while their existence witnesses the cotemporary appreciation of one who used "not dim enigmas doubtful to discern," but expressed himself in "simple truths that every man may learn."* How so prominent a character, overwhelmed with active duties, often in temporary quarters and with few conveniences — but always with assistants about him to perform the manual part of the work — should largely from preference, with his own hand find opportunity to correspond with the Government, its members, governors of States, his generals and officers of every grade, his family and personal friends, the representatives of foreign governments and interests, even with citizens scarcely known to him — but alive to the value of their own wants or suggestions — all with courtesy, uniformity, and neatness, is as remarkable as the variety of the topics and the smallness of the material for subsequent criticism.

These letters collected would seem manually the work of a clerkly copyist rather than originals, the brain and hand work of the founder of a great nation, simply recording, even while creating, much of its history, amidst conflict and doubt. Many of these have found their place in print, all might be condensed with advantage, into a sort of complete letter writer for the use of schools.

With a character naturally strong, developed by a capable and devoted mother, an ordinary education and the adventurous experience of his youth, Washington is marked, by a course of life, ever leading upward and onward. While largely controlling the country he had helped so materially to create, he was ready to entertain and use what he considered adaptable to present circumstances, from the experience of wise men of all periods, refined in the crucible of his own broad common sense.

* Applied from an early poem of William Allen Butler.

Even his conclusions, enforced by such admitted and successful experience, were not always accepted. He had passed to power through triumphal arches raised by a nation's gratitude, to hold it with a people, and even his cabinet, divided as to his policy; and to resign it, and return like Cincinnatus to his plough, with an expressed sense of relief. If so living now, he would be rewarded by the universal thanks of *those familiar with his name and service*, which did not fully attend him, when two factions disputed over his policy, and many beset him from interest or for place. The highest popularity not spasmodic, attending all great men burthened with power and patronage in life, may be claimed to attach to their memory, after they are dead.

If this be so, his parting words when surrendering his highest and final authority — and which probably combined with his own judgment that of others[48] whom his confidence in itself proved also worthy of lasting attention — cannot, it would seem, be too often recalled as embodying past experience, with a far seeing warning for the future, increasing in value as it addresses a larger auditory.

At least an annual public reading of that Farewell Address, with that of the Declaration of Independence — to the fulfillment of the purposes of which it applies — and their study also in our schools, would appear to be necessary instruction to all who may aspire to public place. They show the birth and early progress of the Freedom they are expected to preserve. Some have always referred to them as opening truths which are already new to millions of unfamiliar ears. Those more accustomed to such teachings — could console themselves, if present, with the adage, "a good thing is worth repeating." In them

[48] To Hamilton, Jay, Jefferson and Madison some of its inspirations were due.

every elector once familiar with their spirit would observe, that in traveling too rapidly in an engrossing present, we may leave behind such less recent but indispensible companions in our country's progress, to follow newer and sometimes falser lights.

By such constant recurrence to the grievances the latter recounts against the British Government, each hearer could discover what was renounced by the founders, and whether by any subsequent legislation, we have voluntarily subjected ourselves to any similar burthens.

With this conviction the accompanying, taken from a very rare cotemporary certified copy of the Declaration, more interesting since the damage to the original in its transfer, is inserted.

The Declaration of Independence, appears in effect an ably drawn and dignified recital of grievances imposed by Parliament, and which had become intolerable to a people growing in intelligence and importance. Its incisive tone, and confident assertion, were well calculated to reach an auditory of various interests scattered in thirteen colonies, differing in population, antecedents and interests, and to arouse them to concerted action.

It rejects the further control of the makers of existing laws, while it suggests no substitution of better ones, evidently with the intention of leaving that duty, with the details of Confederate action, to the future representatives of a free people. Its value would appear to be in the position it asserted at a time when the hope of success appeared dark, and in recording the opinion of its patriot founders as to what were then held to be wicked impositions by legislation, under color of law.⁴⁹ " Our present legislation therefore, is subject to a comparison with that of the obnoxious Parliament as there specially denounced, as well as to discover the extent and value of the improvements it is making under the present limit Congress attaches to its power. In this view it may be considered the chart by which the ship of state was expected by them to be navigated. Either to appreciate the history of the details in which that power originated, or its use in the present and future it would appear that education in our past was indispensable to every citizen, and that it was especially the duty of those who inherited their rights from the founders, to qualify themselves not only to understand and protect the enjoyment of the legacy bequeathed to them, free from the effects of any alleged abuses of legislation, but to interest themselves, to arouse a similar sentiment in those who have rapidly joined them. Not to recall as an empty phrase, but to illustrate, that Eternal Vigilance *is* the price of liberty, by observing the proceedings of all bodies acting with delegated power, and if practicable, by wisely influencing the discretion with which that authority is conferred, by the individual citizen.

⁴⁹ These grievances urged against the Bills of Parliament for " the better peopling of the Colonies," in the Congress of 1774, show that England was then charged with transporting a material she desired to be rid of, more dreaded than the " Hessians " so unanimously denounced a few years later. The laws of the Colonies then deprived them of every privilege beyond that of residence.

"That it was too well known that in pursuance of divers Acts of Parliament *great numbers of Fellows who have forfeited their lives to the Public, for the most atrocious crimes, are annually transported from home to these Plantations.* Very surprising, one would think, that *Thieves, Burglars, Pickpockets and Cutpurses*, and a herd of the most flagitious Banditts upon earth should be sent as agreeable companions to us." * * * "But the acts were intended *for the better peopling of the Colonies !* And will thieves and murderers be conductive to that end ? What advantage can we reap from a Colony of unrestrainable Renegadoes ? Will they exalt the glory of the crown ? * * * Can Agriculture be promoted when the wild Boar of the Forest breaks down our Hedges and pulls up our Vines ? * * How injurious

At the present time, with a population swollen by emigration in a single year beyond its great natural increase, by nearly three-quarters of a million, the growing importance of the teaching of history in all our schools would seem to impress itself on all who desire to preserve our integrity. Many are coming to us naturally ignorant of our past and present and its cost to our forefathers and value to us and to them, and who cannot become parts of a homogeneous population advantageously until they have accepted intelligently our institutions in place of those under which they were born, and to which they were possibly hostile, rejecting as impracticable a dual nationality.

A knowledge of American history would appear as requisite as those simple elements of education which enable the elector — and perhaps future ruler — to read an amendment of a constitution, on which by a steady extension of the privileges won in that struggle, he is soon qualified to vote. All details of the past—on a more liberal construction of some of which it is hoped that this use of these papers may possibly throw a ray of additional light, more useful than that of their earlier cremation, which some weary reader may already consider — should be constantly perfected and studied, even amidst the engrossing activity of the present.

_{does it seem to free one part of the Dominions of the Plagues of Mankind and cast them upon another? Should a law be proposed to take the poor of one Parish, and billet them upon another, would not all the world but the parish to be relieved, exclaim against such a project as iniquitous and absurd? Should the numberless Villains of London and Westminister, be suffered to escape from their Prisons, to range at large and depredate any other parts of the Kingdom, would not every man join with the Sufferers and condemn the measures as hard and unreasonable * * * *There are thousands of honest men, laboring in Europe at four pence a day, starving in spite of all their efforts, a dead weight to the respective parishes to which they belong; who without any other qualifications than Common Sense, Health and Strength, might accumulate estates amongst us, as many have done already. These, and not the others, are the men that should be sent over, for the better peopling the Plantations."}

Such information is constantly becoming more valuable to a country wholly unprecedented in history in its absolute reliance upon the patriotism, education, common sense, and mutual concession of its citizens, as a guide for the future, the success of which is necessarily based on such knowledge of the past, on wide spread intelligence, a mutual adaptation, and regard for its founders and its early traditions. If any return were expected, for the labor of compiling and feebly annotating them, beyond an impression that perhaps " the deed in the doing it savors of worth ; " it would be most acceptable in the evidence that they had been the means of impressing upon some earnest reader, the fact, even if controverting one of Mr. Herbert Spencer's theories, that *education only* can open the knowledge of the origin of a nation, inspire a proper pride in its progress and insure its permanency. (Appendix B.)

That intelligence and ignorance have rarely existed long together without one asserting the control. That while some particles of this great aggregate — content to float like the smaller esculant, on the surface of a seething caldron, relying on an exaggerated estimate of their weight, perpetuity and value, by their temporary elevation — above larger roots — may sneer at such researches, as to the truly great men, and the earlier unsuccessful aspirants, long since buried underground ; as unnecessary to uneducated citizenship, and disparaging to spontaneous statesmenship ; it has been the universal testimony of men of broader development and experience, that nothing can give a greater facility to a person of natural capacity, in judging of present events, than the appreciative study of those of the past. He can then discover many old masks on the faces of new actors on the public stage, and that they are often too large for the new wearer. That the best critical analysis applicable to new theories of government, is based upon a knowledge of their success or failure in earlier times.

That few things are on investigation discovered to be purely original, and that many projects have always been sustained by facts, some by fiction, and others by selfish interest. To prepare himself by study, using the ample means supplied for education or reading, would then appear to be the natural means of availing of the privilege every American enjoys. With these we readily discover the relative progress of nations, that where intelligence is habitually developed, it results as a necessity in the prosperity for the many; or where neglected, all others are subordinated to the advantage of the few.

By such research it is easy to discover that there have been many political orators in the country, since the days of Patrick Henry, and many financiers, since Robert Morris, but none who more faithfully devoted available talents to the public. That there have also been many manipulations and fluctuations in finance since their time, in which fortunes changed in ownership, and rulers of the Change rose and fell. That there have been political questions and popular uprisings, involving bitter feeling, and threatening violence, in which the sober, common sense of the country — much of it grounded on the study of the similar crises in the past — has arisen in its might, come to the front, and with a strong hand torn the excited actors apart. It can be seen by reflection that to continue to accomplish this, the body politic must continue in vigorous health. That it demands no less care than in its youth, that like the human system, it requires the healthy circulation of the blood in every organ, to insure vigorous manhood and well preserved longevity.

in the Revolution. 93

That knowledge, equally divided, is the only practicable and lasting communism, and that the crafty demagogue, as a cunning alchemist, with ignorance as the metal to be fused and mingled with rejected theories, proposes a panacea to satisfy the cravings of all, and scatter wealth,[50] without intelligence, industry, or thrift, while he knows that by the substitution of intelligence and education he would in time produce the results to which he claims attention by pretending to seek, but in doing so feels that he must expose the empty charlatanism of a distribution of money without that of the elements that would continue the equality of its division; unless accompanied by that of education and its frequent companion, thrift, valuable qualities calculated to ensure its care and increase.

Those who voluntarily assume the labor and outlay, incurred in the management of those princely private charities, which make New York, even alone, an asylum for the world's unfortunates, can give practical testimony, both as to the immense increasing clientage which presses for relief, and the very large proportion it includes of those who have never profited by those accessories to self protection from chronic destitution. (Appendix C.)

[50] This anecdote of Herrmann the Magician, in a St. Louis newspaper simply illustrates the relative value of many new theories. After reaching the market he walked up to a huckster stand kept by a credulous old German named Mrs. Orf, asking her, as he looked over her stock of provisions, whether the eggs she had on hand were good.

"Yes," replied the old lady, "they are the freshest eggs in the market. If you don't think so just break one and see for yourself."

The magician picked up the egg and broke it open. To her astonishment three ten-dollar gold pieces rolled from the broken shell, which she grabbed at convulsively, *but Herrmann was too quick for her and pocketed the money*, while she gesticulated wildly and insisted that he should return it on the spot. Instead of complying with her request, however, he broke another egg, from which four ten-dollar gold pieces rolled out among the vegetables. This was too much for Mrs. Orf, who told him *to leave instantly as she had no more eggs to waste.*

Dr. Pollock, in a recent essay, has told us that "The ultimate object of natural science is to predict events — to say with approximate accuracy what will happen under given conditions. Every special department of science occupies itself with predicting events of a particular kind; note, also, that each science occupies itself only with those conditions which are material for its own purposes." The laws of science naturally govern both men and nations. While all of their details are too unlimited for the capacity of a single mind, it would appear that each of those controlled by them may realize in his own experience, some valuable developments without assuming to devote himself to any specialty. In a like manner, some study of the rise and progress of government, and of the conditions which have influenced prosperity or decadence, may cause the reader to feel that he is more capable of "predicting events of a particular kind," such as those incident to the homogeneous association of men for the difficult task of government. But, while the study of science may be properly divided, does it not seem that in the constant observation of every detail of the administration of a republican government, where each citizen is equally interested in its safety and success, if not in its control, all should devote their relative capacity, in seeking to apply to it all those principles which have proved to have been " conditions which are material " to perpetuity in former experience, and to reject such errors as have often resulted in national disaster ? [51]

[51] A widely read Journal of the day would appear to confirm the value of uniting the progress of those material "conditions" in enquiring as to those of the great metropolis : "Are there no dangers to-day ? Is the tax levy a myth, with its ten millions for salaries ? Are our officials models of purity, capacity, and fidelity ? Are public works conducted with economy ? Is the administration of municipal affairs prudent and business like ? If so, let us continue to think about reform, after the politicians have arranged the division of the spoils ; let us hold meetings, appoint committees, pass resolutions, after the succession to the lucrative municipal offices has been decided upon."

It is repeating a possibly forgotten truth, that Rome was inwardly the weakest in the zenith of her greatest outward prosperity, " when the sun " it was said " in its whole meridian course kissed her legionary eagles scattered over every clime." That its downfall occurred, when its people, palled by success, became luxurious and enervated, with a growing fondness for the appetible, but enfeebling confections, spread before them by political pastry cooks, and neglected the wholesome diet of substantial facts, on which the Conscript fathers subsisted while erecting the edifice, and which they prescribed for the nourishment of their posterity.

The inference of a matter of fact citizen, when told how " Nero " had "fiddled when Rome was burning," " that he must have been very fond of music to lose so grand a spectacle" might apply to all of us who in neglecting to take an interest in passing events are uninformed to what extent we are excelling Rome in our progress and whether we are avoiding *all* of the errors which finally culminated in her downfall.

Another prosperous one, borne rapidly along by the present luxurious appliances, may only glance upon the Obelisk, impressed with the obligation conferred by its generous gift, and skillful transportation to a new world, and conjecture whether the Egyptian or Roman chariots, it looked down upon for ages after its erection, compared in finish and comfort, with a modern brougham ; but not whether Western Union, Union Pacific, or any other Union, will stand as erect and last as long — through the succession of long dynasties of Ptolemies and Cæsars to that of " City Fathers," without similar care and scientific assistance.

The correspondent at Rome of the "New York Evening Post" recently said " Brescia is still excited by the great theme of

Arnaldo. But we are getting a little too much of this historical archæology. Manuta is preparing to observe the nineteenth centennary of Virgil; Arezzo will soon keep that of Guido Monaco, the inventor of musical notes; Arpim that of Cicero, and Urbino that of Raphael. Some one sagely observes "that instead of studying so intently the history of great Italians dead, it were better to improve the present generation, and expect great deeds from those who live."

Although it is true that Italy has not in later generations equalled those of the past in producing additions to her long line of illustrious names; and that her progress in this has been outstripped by many nations, unborn when she was already grey, it is proper to remember her heavy fall in the race of destiny, and how slow the recovery is.

If the traveler in that classic land still finds himself rather dreaming of her former greatness than awakened to evidences of a new progress, would it not appear that it was therefore more especially needed to recall past triumphs, to inspire in a later generation a spirit of pride, a desire to emulate, and a search for the appliances with which it was secured. At least it would seem natural to us, living in a country unpeopled by civilization at the time when they were wearing its laurels, to feel grateful that we are able to profit by the results of their early labors, which we enjoy in our schools, galleries and industries, and that each remembrance of their name, recalling their example may perhaps inspire imitation of their progress. That in their own land the persistence in thus recording those memories, must with wider educational preparation, in time incite many additional aspirants, to the fame of those whose self erected monuments tower so near them, and still inspire such efforts, in keeping their memory green.

Have not such revivals of the past, often held to be sentimental, a practical use? What reflecting man can pause near that Obelisk without recalling its wierd history, the scenes it has witnessed, and the eyes that have looked upon it in its forty centuries, the changes of faith, dynasties, and conditions of the human race which it records but of which it cannot speak? He may study its rugged silence, read there the history, the progress, vicissitudes and relative perpetuation of men and things, and gain a lesson of the littleness of a single life, which passes away without some honored record, only adding another to the billions who have tread beneath its shadow.

Nearly three-quarters of a century ago Joseph Delaplaine, of Philadelphia, an early appreciator of the association between that ancient republic and our own, then young; at least in the coincidence of the early development of greatness, said—with an uninterrupted flow of enthusiasm — in the prospectus of the "Collection of the Portraits of Distinguished Americans," which still usefully recalls his own name: "With a pride similar to his who, in the mansion of his ancestors, loves to dwell upon the venerable array of their portraits which surrounds him; and, by the almost living glances which dart from the canvas, feels himself unconsciously awed to virtue, will the unborn citizens of this expanding hemisphere, day after day, delight to sojourn amidst the forms of the *fathers of their country*, and depart from the exhibition with newer and stronger aspirations after virtuous renown! 'I have often,' to quote the language of the historian of the Jugurthinian war, 'heard that Quintus Maximus and Publius Scipio, and other illustrious men of our city, were accustomed to declare, when they looked upon the portraits of their ancestors, that they felt their minds most vehemently excited to virtue. Not, indeed, that the impression or the figure produced such powerful effects upon them, but by the recollections of the achievements of these great characters, that a flame was created in their breasts not to be quelled until they should have reached an equal elevation of fame and glory.' 'The history of such men,' says the learned translator of Plutarch, ' is a continuous lesson of practical morality,' and what could be a more pleasing and impressive history of this country than that which would be exhibited in the well-arranged portraits of those by whom its moral and political grandeur was founded and raised to perfection ? The countenance of a Washington would mark the epoch of its military, and of a Franklin of its philosophical glory ; and all the galaxy of genius around them, while furnishing the materials for memory to work upon, *would create new heroes, and stimulate new sages, new statesmen and new orators.*"

"When time shall have swept away the splendid train of our earliest philosophers, statesmen and warriors, to swell the gathering of the grave ; when the tongue of genius shall moulder in gloomy silence ; when the eye of the orator shall be closed in darkness, and the spiritual fires of its glance no longer kindle the dormant intellects around ; when the warrior's arm shall be sinewless, and by the side of his decaying form the sword of his triumphs shall lie rusting ; when the patrons of the soil shall have become an ingredient in its physical amalgama ; *a generous and grateful posterity will rank amongst the first of its public institutions*, that which will afford them, in effects, the delights of a sweet and familiar intercourse with beings endeared to them by the brilliance of their talents, and their virtues, as well as by the benefits which they conferred upon the land of their birth."

Since this enthusiastic patriot thus wrote, with many of his subjects still alive, a large portion of a century has given us better light than he possessed!

Many had then been born under the sway of a government which they once loving, had lived to hate, and doubtless the most modest of those who had aided in its downfall hoped that their names would survive, often recalled in history and the succession of their descendants.[52] They witnessed, as it were, the setting out of a small train, at moderate speed, which we see vastly extended by increase and emigration, wheeling at a terrific speed over a widely extended track. One later accession, that of California, with nearly 189,000 square

[52] Horatio Seymour a life long appreciator and collector, of the records of the achievements of those who opened the way to the many honors have been conferred upon or offered to him, in reply to an invitation to unite in the Bi-Centennial Celebration of the ancient town of Yonkers — a very interesting occasion with which the contributor as an old resident of the neighborhood was gratified in being remembered, in its management — has lately written to its Mayor some valuable truths sustaining these impressions.

"I regret that the state of my health will not allow me to attend the Bi-Centennial Celebration at Phillipse Hall at Yonkers. It is gratifying to learn that throughout our State there is shown a desire to mark with monuments spots of historic interest, and to collect and preserve all things which throw light upon the history of the past.

These things not only show but they create a spirit of patriotism, they give value and interest to the scenes which they mark or illustrate. By them the past speaks to the present. They tell us much of the history of early events; they teach us our duties, and create higher standards of patriotism and virtue.

Monuments, historical societies, and all arrangements to collect and preserve papers and objects relating to the past, not only teach us of the acts and virtues of the dead, but they also show the character of the living and mark the civilization of the people. Monuments in enduring stone have for many centuries been silent but potent teachers of duty and devotion to the public welfare. Even now, after the lapse of many centuries, if their time-worn remains were swept away, the world would feel the loss of objects which remind us of our duties to the public.

Heretofore we have reason to mourn the want of historical collections throughout our State which would show its citizens had a just sense of the great and varied events of its history. This dishonored not the dead but the living. Your celebration, and others of a like character, prove that our citizens are waking up to their duties, and mean to make the public familiar with its events, the most varied and far reaching of any portion of our country."

miles of territory, over 68,000 more than the whole of Great Britain, best illustrates the development of her rebellious child.

By the suppression of the Tory or his departure, by the absorption of those men of figure who then largely owned the colonies or controlled their affairs, by the extension of a limited franchise to one unbounded and unprecedented in its beneficence, by the want of much consideration for family service, in public affairs, and by the omission to a great extent of any veneration for official position, we are all now equals before the law; coequal sovereigns like the old Electors Palatine who chose by vote the Emperor. Still those patriot fathers would seem to be the parents by adoption of every citizen, particularly of those who are coming to wear the crown which they created, at least until by the prosperity open to most who seek it, they in turn, create positions, dating from their birth or arrival in the New World in which each one, equalling the usefulness of those predecessors may claim to be the "Rudolph of Hapsburg" 'of his own family, by contributing as honored a portrait and name as theirs to posterity.

The acquisition of property, gives an additional interest in the nationality to each one who achieves an ownership, however small, and its distribution amongst many in such divisions is the greatest guarantee of perpetuity. A State will be found, in all time, to have been most prosperous, where property was most divided, and where the extremes of the very rich, and the very poor, are exceptional, for the reason that the hundreds of one man by the laws of nature are as valuable to him as the millions of another. But there is a common security under a thoroughly popular form of government, that even the man who owns one dollar, is a stockholder. We watch our investment, in all other securities, and if in stocks study the daily prices. Do we sufficiently realize that they are mere "connections" with the honest administration and prosperity of the government, and exist in its permanency alone? Would it not seem that any vigilance displayed, in the selection of trustees of those lesser securities, with a view to their prosperity and honor, must apply with greater force to that of the government, which is the trunk line.

If a stockholder suspects that his property is controlled by directors forced upon him by bargain and traffic, by primaries to which he has no access, by organizations, machines or rings formed to control the agents and property of any corporation, in the interests of a self-selected few, would he not if he had read of it, conceive that it was in danger of returning to a class government, more dangerous than the one that was annihilated by the Revolution of 1776?

If the air were tainted by the fumes of a conflagration would he not seek for its location and flood it with water for the common good; and if it was filled with nauseous rumors of selfish, and even dishonest combinations, for the control of his corporate property, turn his attention to the necessity of vigilance and of putting trusted parties in its charge? All political history shows that two parties are necessary to a State, each a safety valve to the other, that a community is no sufferer by the parliamentary discussion of questions of policy, where its people differ, but that when such issues are avoided, by the fear of either or both parties, to assume a policy, then there is greater danger in combinations of the worst element in both, for impure and selfish legislation. That all coalitions have been looked upon with doubt, we gather from such history, that the most competent, are often the most modest, in claiming place, while all countries have been supplied with varied voluntary material for office and power from the best, down to such as that which assassinated a president, because a worthless life seemed to him unfitting for reward, as a minister to Austria or consul to Paris!

Doubtless many cultivated readers, versed — as an example — in the teachings of Spencer, Huxley and Tyndall, perhaps from the absence of an appreciative taste, disregard the lessons of that history, of which most men, are unknowingly forming part, either by action or its neglect. All concede the value of patriotism, many are often critical as to its presence as an impulse; possibly few consider that merely as an accomplishment it can be acquired by the study of its many results, or of the effects of its absence. A less cultivated but patriotic and shrewd observer like Mrs. Grundy—whose views have often become the reflex of public opinion—is in many cases more useful, than a more learned perfunctionary and statistical manipulator. (Appendix D.)

In complying with his promise to the editor, the contributor has sought, in adding some material connected with his undertaking, to incidentally consider our progress in the eradication of the complaints against the government on which we were founded, and the uses we were making of a wonderful legacy, by following past history.

That gentleman's thoughtful note, at the end of his own contribution — as to the difficulties under which they have been loosely thrown together, gives the opportunity to say that he has neither seen the manuscript, nor is he responsible for its contents, its contribution being purely voluntary.

Not happening to have met either himself or General de Peyster since it was undertaken, and having no knowledge of what the latter had contributed to this accidentally triple association, he fears that in his friendly desire to aid in his natura effort to vindicate the memory of his relative, he may have repeated or controverted some of the views, which he has doubtless, with his usual independency, asserted. In either such event, it has been his object to express the sympathy study teaches to humanity, as to the unfortunate fate and hardships of the Loyalists. In doing this he does not feel that he detracts from his own fealty to the government formed on their ruin, in which it is his pride to have been bred to feel the responsibility of aiding to hand it down, as a home of freedom wisely administered, to future generations. This explanation appears proper to account for any apparent want of cohesion, or accord, in the expression of individual, and therefore possibly conflicting opinion, in arriving at a common purpose, of recalling the memory of historical characters.

On a final reading of this contribution, it suggests some resemblance to a trunk hastily packed for a journey, with an opportunity for selection from a sufficient wardrobe, which when resorted to, is found to contain some articles better fitted for the seclusion of a private apartment, than for public use, and to lack, many others more adaptable, but improvidently left at home.

SPRING HOUSE, RICHFIELD,
September, 1882.

APPENDIX A.

COL. GUY JOHNSON'S LETTER (page 77).

◂●●●▸

The following letter from Col. Guy Johnson to his uncle, is also found in Dr. Emmett's collection. It gives some particulars illustrative of the surroundings of both.

N. York, Feby. 10, 1773.

My dear Sir William,

I have just now had the pleasure of receiving your very kind letter of the 3d inst., with one from Dr. Dease*, another from Brother Claus, for which I am much obliged to them. It has vexed me a good deal to hear that your Votes did not go up early. They went by John Glen, and Gaine† assures me he has forwarded a sett since. As the titles of several bills are altered in the Committees, it may be necessary to acquaint you that the Road bill and money bill for building a Ct. House, &c., are passed through every form and the Tavern Bill, Swine Bill, Wolf Bill and Ferry Bill, will be in a very few days. You will find me voting on a side that some people might not expect. It will all be accounted for in due time, but is chiefly owing to certain difficulties imposed on the Governor. The other day they were for saddling a £50 per annum Salary, on the Judges of Circuit, to be paid out of our County, but after much difficulty, I got it laid general on the Province, Major Skene‡ is just going for Ireland. He has the other day got his place established as the County town. The Pacquet is arrived. All Peace at home. The General has got the King's leave to go to England, and will sail in June with his family. Haldemand§ comes to take the command; and Governor Tryon (it is said) will have the vacant Red Ribband. He has taken much pains about the Indian matters, Banyar‖ advises to get an Act for Fairs and Markets in lieu of the Ordinance, but the Governor choses the latter. In the Charter for the Church a description of the Glebe is absolutely necessary and how the right presentation should go. I hope you

---

* Dr. John Dease was an Executor and Trustee under Sir William's will.
† Hugh Gaine, editor of the *New York Mercury*, printed in Hanover Square; established in 1752.
‡ Col. Philip Skene was settled at Skenesborough (now Whitehall), and was actively employed by Burgoyne in his Invasion.
§ Gen. Gage came in lieu of Haldimand.
‖ Goldsboro Banyar.

will continue your Parental attention to Polly and the little ones, she is I believe surprised I stay so long and I eagerly wish to return. The girls are well and much esteemed. The like may be said with great truth of Sir John. He will return with me and doubtless lay before you, the final determination of the Family here, respecting his union which I see nothing to prevent. The lady* is a fine Genteel Girl, much esteemed as well on acco't of the goodness of her Temper, as of her uncommon abilities, and she is ready to follow him anywhere.

The man calls for my Letter, so that I can only beg a continuance of your correspondence, which yields me much real pleasure, and assure you once more of the Cordial Wishes I offer for your Health and happiness, and the true Affection with which I subscribe myself,
My dear Sir,
Your dutiful son and faithful servant,
G. JOHNSON.[†]

Sir Wm. Johnson, Bt.

APPENDIX B.

MR. HERBERT SPENCER'S FIRST IMPRESSIONS OF AMERICA
(page 91).

The immense progress of America, attracting the attention of Europe, makes it the field for that observing travel, long confined to the seats of departed greatness. The Emperor of Brazil, Petermann, Nordenskjöld and a Baker Pacha, all notable in exploration, Hughes, Dean Stanley, Thackeray, Dickens, observers of character, the Prince of Wales, and Alexis and the Duke of Argyle, have come to us in late years; others are following, some of them less known but fully as competent, to view and estimate its reputed greatness. Dr. Mackenzie, an eminent specialist of London, has recently made a wide, rapid and intelligent exploration, and is now succeeded by Herbert Spencer, noted for the independence with which he has often asserted advanced ideas on questions intended to affect humanity. He who looks at himself in a glass, often derives a different impression from that of another, who disinterestedly criticises a portrait satisfactory to the owner. An interview, given to the public since the foregoing crude inferences were printed,[‡] and arriving in some

---

* Miss Mary Watts, daughter of John Watts, Esq., of New York, to whom Sir John was married on the 30th of June following.
[†] Col. Guy Johnson was then a new Member of the Colonial Assembly. See Stone's "Sir William Johnson," vol. 2, page 359.
[‡] *New York Times*, Oct. 20th.

cases at different conclusions, appears to be an unfinished sketch worthy to be hung by the side of the completed picture, to which Delaplaine referred. If in expressing his views, as a humanitarian, upon the progress of a sapling torn from the royal oak, any impression of national jealousy is suggested, is it not well to recall the truthful adage "fas est et ab hoste doceri." Mr. Spencer, with the appreciation wanting in the Obelisk, and with some of its experience derived from study of progressive races and their development. After speaking of inferential facts, being asked:

"Might not this misrepresentation have been avoided by admitting interviewers?" replies,

"Possibly; but, in the first place, I have not been sufficiently well; and, in the second place, I am averse to the system. To have to submit to cross examination, under penalty of having ill natured things said if one refuses, is an invasion of personal liberty which I dislike. Moreover, there is implied what seems to me an undue love of personalities. Your journals recall a witticism of the poet Heine, who said that 'when a woman writes a novel, she has one eye on the paper and the other on some man — except the Countess Hahn-hahn, who has only one eye.' In like manner, it seems to me that in the political discussions that fill your papers, everything is treated in connection with the doings of individuals — some candidate for office, or some "boss" or wire-puller. I think it not improbable that this appetite for personalties, among other evils, generates this recklessness of statement. The appetite must be ministered to; and in the eagerness to satisfy its cravings, there comes less and less care respecting the correctness of what is said."

"Has what you have seen answered your expectations?"

"It has far exceeded them. Such books about America as I had looked into had given me no adequate idea of *the immense developments of material civilization* which I have everywhere found. The extent, wealth, and magnificence of your cities, and especially the splendor of New York, have altogether astonished me. Though I have not visited the wonder of the West, Chicago, yet some of your minor modern places, such as Cleveland, have sufficiently amazed me by the marvelous results of one generation's activity. Occasionally, when I have been in places of some 10,000 inhabitants, where the telephone is in general use, I have felt somewhat ashamed of our own unenterprising towns, many of which of 50,000 inhabitants and more, make no use of it."

"I suppose you recognize in these results the great benefit of free institutions?"

"Ah, now comes one of the inconveniences of interviewing. I have been in the country less than two months, have seen but a relatively small part of it, and but comparatively few people, and yet you wish from me a definite opinion on a difficult question."

"Perhaps you will answer, subject to the qualification that you are but giving your first impressions?"

Well, with that understanding, I may reply that, though free institutions have been partly the cause, I think they have not been the chief cause. In the first place, the American people have come into possession of an unparalled fortune — the mineral wealth and the vast tracts of virgin soil producing abundantly with small cost of culture. Manifestly that alone goes a long way toward producing this enormous prosperity. Then they have profited by inheriting all the arts, appliances, and methods developed by older societies, while leaving behind the obstructions existing in them. They have been able to pick and choose from the products of all past experience, appropriating the good and rejecting the bad. Then, besides these favors of fortune, there are factors proper to themselves. I perceive in American faces generally, a great amount of determination — a kind of "do or die" expression; and this trait of character, joined with a power of work exceeding that of any other people, of course produces an unparalleled rapidity of progress. Once more, there is the inventiveness which stimulated by the need for economizing labor, has been so wisely fostered. Among us in England there are many foolish people who while thinking that a man who toils with his hands has an equitable claim to the product, and if he has special skill may rightly have the advantage of it, also hold that if a man toils with his brain, perhaps for years, and, uniting genius with perseverance, evolves some valuable invention, the public may rightly claim the benefit. The Americans have been more far-seeing. The enormous museum of patents which I saw at Washington is significant of the attention paid to inventors' claims, and the Nation profits immensely from having in this direction (though not in all others) recognized property in mental products. Beyond question, in respect of mechanical appliances, the Americans are ahead of all nations. If along with your material progress there went equal progress of a higher kind, there would remain nothing to be wished."

"That is an ambiguous qualification. What do you mean by it?"

"You will understand when I tell you what I was thinking of the other day. After pondering over what I have seen of your vast manufacturing and trading establishments, the rush of traffic in your street cars and elevated railways, your gigantic hotels and Fifth-avenue palaces, I was suddenly reminded of the Italian republics of the Middle Ages, and recalled the fact that while there was growing up in them great commercial activity, a development of the arts which made them the envy of Europe, and a building of princely mansions which continue to be the admiration of travelers, their people were gradually losing their freedom."

"Do you mean this as a suggestion that we are doing the like?"

"It seems to me that you are. You retain the forms of freedom, but so far as I can gather, there has been a considerable loss of the substance. It is true that *those who rule you* do not do it by means of retainers armed with swords; but they do it through regiments of men armed with voting-papers, who obey the word of command as loyally as did the dependents of the old feudal nobles, and who thus enable their leaders to override the general will and make the community submit to their exactions as effectually as their prototypes of old. It is doubtless true that each of your citizens votes for the candidate he chooses for this or that office from President downward, but his hand is guided by a power behind, which leaves him scarcely any choice. 'Use your political power as we tell you, or else throw it away,' is the alternative offered to the citizen. The political machinery as it is now worked has little resemblance to that contemplated at the outset of your political life. Manifestly, those who framed your Constitution never dreamed that 10,000 citizens would go to the poll led by a "boss." America exemplifies, at the other end of the social scale, a change analogous to that which has taken place under sundry despotisms. You know that in Japan, before the recent revolution, the divine ruler, the Mikado, nominally supreme, was practically a puppet in the hands of his chief Minister the Shogun. Here it seems to me that the 'sovereign people' is fast becoming a puppet which moves and speaks as wire-pullers determine."

"Then you think that republican institutions are a failure."

"By no means! I imply no such conclusion. Thirty years ago, when often discussing politics with an English friend, and defending republican institutions, as I always have done and do still; and when he urged against me the ill-working of such institutions over here; I habitually replied that the Americans got their form of government by a happy accident, not by normal progress, and that they would have to go back before they could go forward. What has since happened seems to me to have justified that view ; and what I see now confirms me in it. America is showing on a larger scale than ever before that ' paper constitutions ' will not work as they are intended to work. The truth, first recognized by Mackintosh, that ' constitutions are not made, but grow,' which is part of the larger truth that societies throughout their whole organizations are not made but grow at once, when accepted, disposes of the notion that you can work, as you hope, any artificially devised system of government. It becomes an inference that if your political structure has been manufactured, and not grown, it will forthwith begin to grow into something different from that intended — something in harmony with the natures of citizens and the conditions under which the society exists. And it evidently has been so with you. Within the forms of your Constitution there has grown up this organization of professional politicians, altogether uncontemplated at the outset, which has become in large measure the ruling power."

"But will not education and the diffusion of political knowledge fit men for free institutions ?"

"No. It is essentially a question of character, and only in a secondary degree a question of knowledge. But for the universal delusion about education as a panacea for political evils, this would have been made sufficiently clear by the evidence daily disclosed in your papers. Are not the men who officer and control your Federal, State, and municipal organizations — who manipulate your caucusses and conventions, and run your partisan campaigns — all educated men ? And has their education prevented them from engaging in or permitting, or condoning, the briberies, lobbyings, and other corrupt methods which vitiate the actions of your administrations ? Perhaps party newspapers exaggerate these things; but what am I to make of the testimony of your civil service reformers — men of all parties ? If I understand the matter aright, they are attacking, as vicious and dangerous, a system which has grown up under the natural spontaneous working of your free institutions — are exposing vices which education has proved powerless to prevent."

"Of course, ambitious and unscrupulous men will secure the offices, and education will aid them in their selfish purposes ; but would not those purposes be thwarted, and better government secured, by raising the standard of knowledge among the people at large ?"

"Very little. The current theory is that if the young are taught what is right, and the reasons why it is right, they will do what is right when they grow up. But, considering what religious teachers have been doing these 2,000 years, it seems to me that all history is against the conclusion, as much as is the conduct of these well educated citizens I have referred to, and I do not see why you expect better results among the masses. Personal interests will sway the men in the ranks as they sway the men above them, and the education which fails to make the last consult public good rather than private good will fail to make the first do it. The benefits of political purity are so general and remote, and the profit to each individual so inconspicuous, that the common citizen, educate him as you like, will habitually occupy himself with his personal affairs, and hold it not worth his while to fight against each abuse as soon as it appears. Not lack of information, but lack of certain moral sentiments, is the root of the evil."

"You mean that people have not a sufficient sense of public duty ?"

"Well, that is one way of putting it ; but there is a more specific way. Probably it will suprise you if I say that the American has not, I think, a sufficiently quick sense of his own claims, and, at the same time, as a necessary consequence, not a sufficiently quick sense of the claims of others — for the two traits are organically related. I observe that you tolerate various small interferences and dictations which

Englishmen are prone to resist. I am told that the English are remarked on for their tendency to grumble in such cases; and I have no doubt that it is true."

"Do you think it worth while for people to make themselves disagreeable by resenting every trifling aggression? We Americans think it involves too much loss of time and temper and doesn't pay."

"Exactly. That is what I mean by character. It is this easy going readiness to permit small trespasses because it would be troublesome or profitless or unpopular to oppose, which leads to the habit of acquiescence in wrong and the decay of free institutions. Free institutions can be maintained only by citizens, each of whom is instant to oppose every illegitimate act, every assumption of supremacy, every official excess of power, however trivial it may seem. As Hamlet says, there is such a thing as 'greatly to find quarrel in a straw' when the straw implies a principle. If, as you say of the American, he pauses to consider whether he can afford the time and trouble — 'whether it will pay '— corruption is sure to creep in. All these lapses from higher to lower forms begin in trifling ways, and it is only by incessant watchfulness that they can be prevented. As one of your early statesmen said: "The price of liberty is eternal vigilance." But it is far less against foreign aggressions upon national liberty that this vigilance is required than against the insidious growth of domestic interferences with personal liberty. In some private administrations which I have been concerned with, I have often insisted, much to the disgust of officials, that instead of assuming, as people usually do, that things are going right until it is proved that they are going wrong, the proper course is to assume that they are going wrong until it is proved that they are going right. You will find, continually, that private corporations, such as joint-stock banking companies, come to grief from not acting upon this principle. And what holds of these small and simple private administrations, holds still more of the great and complex public administrations. People are taught, and, I suppose, believe, that 'the heart of man is deceitful above all things and desperately wicked;' and yet, strangely enough, believing this, they place implicit trust in those they appoint to this or that function. I do not think so ill of human nature; but, on the other hand, I do not think so well of human nature as to believe it will do without being watched."

"You hinted that while Americans do not assert their own individualties sufficiently in small matters, they, reciprocally, do not sufficiently respect the individualities of others."

"Did I? Here, then, comes another of the inconveniences of interviewing. I should have kept this opinion to myself if you had asked me no questions, and now I must either say what I do not think, which I cannot, or I must refuse to answer, which, perhaps, will be taken to mean more than I intend, or I must specify at the risk of giving offense. As the least evil I suppose I must do the last. The trait I refer to comes out in various ways, small and great. It is shown by the disrespectful manner in which individuals are dealt with in your journals — the placarding of public men in sensational headings, the dragging of private people and their affairs into print. There seems to be a notion that the public have a right to intrude on private life as far as they like; and this I take to be a kind of moral trespassing. It is true that during the last few years we have been discredited in London by certain weekly papers which do the like (except in the typographical display); but in our daily press, metropolitan and provincial, there is nothing of the kind. Then, in a larger way, the trait is seen in this damaging of private property by your elevated railways without making compensation; and it is again seen in the doings of railway governments, not only when overriding the rights of shareholders, but in dominating over courts of justice and State governments. The fact is that free institutions can be properly worked only by men each of whom is jealous of his own rights, and also sympathetically jealous of the rights of others — will neither himself aggress on his neighbors, in small things or great, nor tolerate aggression on them by others. The Republican form of Government is the highest form of Government, but because of this it requires the highest type of human nature — a type nowhere at present existing. We have not grown up to it, nor have you."

"But we thought, Mr. Spencer, you were in favor of free government in the sense of relaxed restraints, and letting men and things very much alone — or what is called *laissez faire?*

"That is a persistent misunderstanding of my opponents. Everywhere, along with the reprobation of government intrusion into various spheres where private activities should be left to themselves, I have contended that in its special sphere, the maintenance of equitable relations among citizens, governmental action should be extended and elaborated."

"To return to your various criticisms, must I then understand that you think unfavorably of our future?"

"No one can form anything more than vague and general conclusions respecting your future. The factors are too numerous, too vast, too far beyond measure in their quantities and intensities. The world has never before seen social phenomena at all comparable with those presented in the United States. A society spreading over enormous tracts while still preserving its political continuity, is a new thing. This progressive incorporation of vast bodies of immigrants of various bloods has never occurred on such a scale before. Large empires, composed of different people, have, in previous cases, been formed by conquest and annexation. Then your immense plexus of railways and telegraphs tends to consolidate this vast aggregate of States in a way that no such aggregate has ever before been consolidated. And there are many minor co-operating causes unlike those hitherto known. No one can say how it is all going to work out. That there will come hereafter troubles of various kinds, and very grave ones, seems highly probable; but all nations have had, and will have, their troubles. Already you have triumphed over one great trouble, and may reasonably hope to triumph over others. It may, I think, be reasonably held that both because of its size and the heterogeneity of its components, the American nation will be a long time in evolving its ultimate form, but that its ultimate form will be high. One great result is, I think, tolerably clear. From biological truths it is to be inferred that the eventual mixture of the allied varieties of the Aryan race forming the population, will produce a more powerful type of man than has hitherto existed, and a type of man more plastic, more adaptable, more capable of undergoing the modifications needful for complete social life. I think that whatever difficulties they may have to surmount, and whatever tribulations they may have to pass through, the Americans may reasonably look forward to a time when they will have produced a civilization grander than any the world has known." Could this be so, were educated citizens largely in the majority, equally fitted to contend at the polls for a number of places necessarily limited in proportion to those who would seek them? Would the intense national individuality, when more widely educated then readily aggregate — as is correctly stated — by thousands, and delegate their power to any single man? Would not the competition of increased intelligence for office, govern success more by fitness, and cause a net to be drawn, with closer meshes over our political sea? On the solution of such questions the permanancy of actual government of the people, *by the people* hinges.

APPENDIX C.

INEVITABLE EFFECTS OF A RAPID PROGRESS ON THE POSITION OF REPRESENTATIVES OF EARLIER SETTLERS (page 93).

These institutions, involving and receiving great attention, and usually conducted with marked integrity and system, naturally include in their management, material as broad as their object. In many of them, may be prominently found the descendants of the original Dutch and English settlers, now rarely met with in the record of public trusts. Their influence and control, has mainly become gradually limited to these, and to their social and business connections, in private life. Any distinct influence, as a recognized or cohesive element, often found in communities, has been lost in the mighty wave of emigration and its increase, which where aggregated controls the selection of most of its representatives. This is more evident at points near to the place of its arrival, and it is necessarily free from the influence of such earlier tradition, and sentiment, as it may in time create in its own successors. Investigation developes such changes of authority in all history, as continuous as the rolling waves sometimes reaching the beach, at others breaking too early, from their acquired force. Under other institutions they are more frequently the result of conquest than of a friendly acceptance with unlimited legal hospitality, as an element of control. When Charles II — claiming under the exploration of the Cabots, in their second voyage in 1497, from their touching the mainland — presented a Dutch colony which he had never possessed, to his brother, the Duke of York, and it was conquered by his agent, Colonel Nicolls in August, 1664, the inhabitants were not only protected in all their rights, by that humane commander, but retained many local positions of authority, after the invasion. Its capture, caused a war between England and the Dutch Provinces, through which a William the Stadtholder of Holland, gradually developed as future King of England, and the loss of a colony by the Dutch was then compensated by the gaining of a crown by a Dutchman. That war was at its origin considered an ungrateful return for the kindness which both of those Princes had experienced when in exile, from the authorities of the Netherlands, unawed by Cromwell's displeasure. Colonel Nicolls, apparently infinitely superior to his master, was killed in a sea fight in that war in 1672, on the Duke of York's ship, while still remembered with affection here by those whom he had subdued. His munificent patron had rewarded him with a gift of £200! on surrendering his difficult and well administered Governorship. Before that conquest, England's early colonies about Nieu Amsterdam — some of them under its sufferance — had been a source of apprehension to its burghers. Their original institutions seemed to have been compassed by the example of their original home, and not to have been adapted to the early extension of that toleration in their new one, to those who had fled to America to secure the liberty of conscience, the struggle for which had long desolated the Low Countries in Europe. All then visiting Nieu Amsterdam, the Dutch Records inform us, became subject to this rule "beside the Reformed Religions, no conventicles shall be holden in houses, barns, ships, woods or fields, under penalty of 50 guilders for each person, man, woman or child attending, for the first offence, double for the second, quadruple for the third, and, arbitrary correction for every other." This early exclusiveness was perhaps an omen of their own later exclusion to a great extent from the control of the public affairs of that ancient settlement once the seat of an almost universal prosperity and a type of practical "Home Rule" in the frugal and primitive administration of its public affairs. Of the six hundred grants for Manors and Estates, once held by them, a small portion remains in the possession of their descendants, if unoccupied, a heavy burthen, by the extravagant and often useless and premature assessments and onerous taxes constantly imposed upon it, in the employment of the labor of those *detained* by the small proportion of the outlay it receives, from an infinitely larger and more lasting reward, in the wide and bountiful field for its occupation in the less crowded Western territory.

Perhaps in time, some humane system may be discovered, to advise new comers of the inevitable law of supply and demand which controls the location of their probable success, and that it is governed by the area open for largely agricultural employment. The "Commissioners of Emigration" have reported a pleasant fact for the Western States: That two-thirds of the emigration, including the most provident, join them directly, led by that intelligence which perhaps had caused such former success, while one third lingers on the sea-board, to compete for employment in crowded and expensive cities, causing the over competition often complained of, and in business revulsions accumulated distress.

APPENDIX D.

MRS. GRUNDY'S OBSERVATIONS AS TO UTOPIA (page 102).

In her recent "Observations in Utopia," Mrs. Grundy, as active as extended in her travels and researches, points out many defects in the administration of that model Republic as instructive to our own. She tells us how "Colonel Trusty, a watchful consul in Switzerland reported — and perhaps violated the rules of the department, in also disclosing, what every intelligent citizen has long known to apply to many nationalities and cities of Europe — that some of the Cantons of Switzerland were shipping their convicts to Utopia, and suggested that an inspection for such contraband of peace, be made at the time of departure, to which no respectable passenger could apparently object. When some compatriots evidently without appreciation that every country has proved able to produce more criminals than its prosperity requires, remonstrated, a junior official replied, that the consul had been reprimanded, and were he not a meritorious veteran would be removed. Would it not be fair, in the absence of any evidence of the pressure of this intelligence upon the earliest Congress for action, to infer that the country *did* desire an accession of such criminals to the honest portion of its citizenship, and their closer proximity to their homes and families. Could this vital suggestion have been overlooked, especially by that successor who had first excelled even, the founder of this Republic in a temperate and frugal denial in the viands of the executive table, and had displayed his unparalled clemency in restoring to rank so many dispensed with for its neglect by the judgment of their fellow officers — always a painful duty.

With a vast area of territory yet to be occupied, the quality as well as the extent of new accessions would seem to interest every citizen. The outrages daily recorded, rarely prove when investigated to be the acts of settled residents but generally of those of a floating and fungus growth who prefer to eat the grapes rather than to labor in the vineyard. Robbery, generally attended by the use of arms and often by the shedding of blood, does not seem to be deterred by the fear of a short and relatively comfortable confinement, with the hope of escape or pardon, by the influence of those perhaps more ready to overlook the wrongs of others, than they would be their own. The shooting of two policemen, at early evening, in a frequented village, while attempting to arrest three successful burglars, loaded with plunder secured in a neighboring town, within the writer's hearing, recalls the value of the Consul's suggestion, and the possibility of these very criminals, being of those he attempted to exclude; an apparently less effective inspection at landing has since been legalized."

"Can the thought be entertained, that with our Washington at the head of government, and substantially the "Father of his Country" he would if advised of it have neglected this warning, as to what would appear to affect the healthy development of any country."

"It would be interesting, if it were possible," she adds, "to hear the criticism of some modern legislation here, and the tracing of its results, by one of our own time honored statesmen — Benjamin Franklin for example — accustomed to be driven from place to place of meeting, legislating with a halter in plain view in case of failure, and surrounded by the hardships of war, and the need of means for its progress, yet with the whole country's best interests always steadily in view. It might provoke even him to mirth, to foreshadow that refinement of push pole navigation, coming as one of the results of a progress based on those sacrifices, when a "constituency" here would demand, in the face of the President's veto, an appropriation to render a stream navigable, which, on a careful inspection proved capable of being carried, in the dry season, in a box drain a foot square. It would have pleased him as a broad philanthropist, to know, that in a recent bill, a provision requiring such inspection hereafter, was a desirable feature, and probably still more so to learn that the value of the method resorted to in the State of New York, of vetoing sections in a bill, and so preserving the interests of proper subjects of legislation had suggested itself also to this Utopian Congress."

"Could so wise a patriot as Franklin, with such intelligence as he had necessarily acquired as to the material of war, have been expected to vote for example, for the

Utopian Pension Act, or other even humane legislation, not limited by provisions for the strictest personal examination of the claimant, by a responsible officer, supplied with ample evidence of identity and service, with power to test the common assertion that conjectured widows, have claimed in the names of soldiers, they have never seen, long lying in honored graves, and that constructive veterans possibly disabled by a bunion, acquired in too hastily retiring from active service, after the receipt of a bounty, are now in a large number of cases subsisting on an equal allowance with actual veterans."

"In our own country Adjutant General Stryker, of New Jersey, a zealous officer, who presents his resignation to each incoming Governor, and is never permitted to surrender a small salary for a large service, has, with much labor from scant State archives by exhaustive search, with little assistance, and small expense, condensed a roster of the Revolutionary service of every contribution from that fighting little State, from a major general to a wagoner. He has supplemented it, with a similar record of service in the last war, and in its inspection the long lists of "deserted," probably mainly of those who never intended to serve — mingled with longer ones of gallant veterans, many of whom fell in battle — is a source of surprise to the reader. I have suggested the preparation and use of such works here. Probably these desertions are not in excess of those of other states, in proportion to their population, but they would be a large numeral addition to the Subsistence Roll of an army. Such records for all the States would seem to be invaluable to a conscientious Pension Agent, or a vigilant investigator of fraudulent bounties or claims. They would be read with attention in Utopia."

"The action of the Viking of Bashwash, when in charge of the Naval Affairs of Utopia, in restoring to the school under control of his Department, a number of cadets who had resigned to avoid an investigation, under charges unfitting them if proved, for service as officers, was greatly disapproved by those who wished to continue to be proud of their Navy, and that of the honored Commander who in strongly protesting, lost the favor of his chief and even his official courtesies, as highly praised." She further says, "the latest amendment to the Constitution of Utopia, which was not passed without opposition, seems worthy of attention. It provides, that every citizen in demanding or collecting interest, rent or any other source of revenue, shall be hereafter required to exhibit to the person of whom payment is asked, at the time of such demand, a certificate to the fact that the creditor had voted at the last election, to be duly certified by the clerk of the Poll, or official evidence of a reasonable excuse, and all debtors, are forbidden to pay without such exhibition. It has already greatly increased the vote of that reserved class, who have heretofore neglected the control of their most valuable investment, by which all others are protected and guaranteed, while attentive to the election of corporate Directors."

"'Civil Service Reform,' is growing in favor with many, from the *liberal* construction of the law. Examinations for appointments are influenced as to their extent by the circumstances. Where *strong* testimonials are presented, they are held to make a searching series of questions as to capacity, unnecessary, but in their absence greater care is considered necessary.

The intention of the law is construed to be to enable the government to avail itself of the services of those whose armor has been hacked and broken in the defence of the interests of the party entrusted with the management of public affairs, and to dispense with the services of good men too engrossed in their duties to give sufficient attention to the interests of the power which protects them.

Their influence, as examples of good citizenship is considered more useful, when scattered unhampered by office amongst the body of the people."

"It is rumored that an effort will be made at the next session of the Utopian Congress, to rescind its novel rule requiring the insertion of pellets of cotton in the ears of a member addressing the chair, after ten minutes speaking, with a view to confining the length of his remarks to the suggestions of the mind, and not to allow them to be led on by the pleasant music of the voice, after the material suggestions have been made. Its intention was to economize valuable time, where all speeches may be elaborated and printed."

"The descendants of the Liberators of Utopia are rarely found in official position. They comfort themselves by feeling that like Alcibiades they may be 'esteemed too just.'

Great attention is given by the farmers here to the breeding of blooded stock, and fabulous prices are paid for animals of approved pedigree."

"This letter from a candidate for the Utopian Congress to the committee who had the power to nominate him; and to their credit did so, has been much discussed, its candor questioned, and its contents pronounced as "toffy," but it has been doubted, largely by those who had spoiled their digestion by its excessive use. Others consider that it is a good old fashioned doctrine."

"Still, that there may be no possibility of mistake, and in simple fairness to the gentlemen who have the matter in control, I take this public way of saying with as much emphasis as may be, that from careful observation and a somewhat intimate acquaintance with the inner workings of both the great political parties, I am convinced that the one greatest curse of our political system is the corrupt use of money and patronage in elections. Were I nominated, I should not directly or indirectly, pay or cause to be paid one dollar to secure an election. Further than this, I may say that, believing the work of office seeking, place brokerage, and position peddling to be no part of the duty of a member of Congress, I should, if elected, refuse positively to take any part in the general scramble for places in the departments, an occupation which can only be engaged in by neglecting legitimate and necessary work in the house at the sacrifice of self-respect, and to the serious detriment and disgrace of the public service. In short, I could only accept the nomination with the distinct understanding that, in addition to earnestly and sincerely subscribing to all the time-honored principles of my party, I should enter the canvass upon the clean new platform of honest, progressive, and independent Republicans. If there be any gentleman who would vote for my nomination on other terms, I beg him to refrain from doing so. His action could only result in disappointment." He was defeated.

It may occur to some weary reader, why some of these notes, apparently disconnected from the subject, are worked in to his annoyance. Simply because it appears that the use made by any nationality, of discussion of the action of either or all of its former rulers, is the strongest censure that can be inflicted by their posterity on those who opposed its creation, and questioned its future integrity, where so many were to be trusted with its control.

Mr. Henry George, who has lately bearded the British Lion in his den, and contended with the Dragon which prevented the universal prosperity and happiness of the human race, as fearlessly as did his namesake, the patron saint of the now oppressors, has on his return hastily plucked a handful of feathers, principally exotic, from the terminal portion of the Utopian "Bird of Freedom." He alludes truthfully, to the extravagance and uncleanliness of "Outre Mer," its great maritime and again largely colonial city, and yet displays an apparent want of appreciation of the causes requisite to the value of his undertaking. He says no one:

"Can go to Europe and study the system of government there without feeling a very great contempt for it — without feeling that he would like to go as a missionary among those people, to tell them to stand up, to teach them the virtues and the beauties and the philosophy of democracy. (Applause.) One thing, however, would deter him. A man would feel like that, if he knew nothing of the condition of this country. He would be met with the suggestion, however, that he look to his own country — to cities like this great metropolis of yours ruled and robbed by a class of miserable politicians."

After stating that if Utopia had been "true of Democratic principles" there would, not now, in his opinion "be a crowned head in Europe," he honestly points out as causes of the delay.

"But what shall we say when over here, where every man is equal before the law, where every citizen has a right to vote, where all power is in the hands of the people, the masses of the workers are but little, if any, better off than on the other side? What is the use of democratic institutions to men who cannot get a living without cringing and buying and selling their manhood. (Applause.) Can we prate and boast of our institutions when we read of people dying of starvation? when we have alms-houses in every city?"

He proposes to exempt improved property from future taxation, but to remove the field for the harvest of the enormous amount of its expenses to the unoccupied portions of the island, and annexed adjacent territory. Speaking of a friend who desired to invest in improvements, he says:

"If he went to the upper portion of this island, as he probably would go, he would find there plenty of vacant land that is now of no use to anybody save as the receptacle of rubbish and a browsing place for goats of that species popularly supposed to live on old boots and glass bottles. Very naturally he would say, no one is using this land. It is, in fact, in its present condition an eyesore and a nuisance. Let me come on it and I will erect a fine house, which will be an ornament to the neighborhood and an inducement to other people to erect good houses in the vicinity. Or I will build a factory in which I will employ a great number of hands, and turn out every year a large amount of goods that everybody desires. Should we not say to him: — 'Go ahead and welcome! Fine houses are better than rubbish-filled lots, and we would rather have factories than goat pastures?' But we say nothing of the kind."

"On the contrary, Mr. Saunders would be confronted by some one by legal right of a title derived from some of the old Dutchmen who first settled this island and who have been dead and gone long years ago, who would say to him, 'Before you can build your houses or erect your factory you must pay me such and such a sum.' Finding that he could not in any other way get a place upon which to make the improvement he contemplated, Mr. Saunders would probably consent to pay a price which, in its nature, would be nothing more nor less than a species of blackmail levied upon a man who wished to improve natural opportunities for the benefit of some dog-in-the-manger who could not and would not use them for himself. His capital being thus further diminished he would proceed to build his house and erect his factory. What then? As soon as he got them up, along would come a tax gatherer and would say to him, you have built a house, you have erected a factory, and for doing these things the laws of this country fine you to such and such an amount, and unless you pay the fine and keep on paying the fine, we will take from you the property which is the result of your exertions.' And not satisfied with that, if Mr. Saunders' skill and prudence and energy enabled him, after all this, to make money, and his providence enabled him to lay it up, the taxgatherer would hunt him up in all sorts of ways and demand new fines and fresh penalties.

"Now, what I contend is, that it is stupid in us to thus hamper and vex and fine the men who enrich our city and our country, and that when we want money for common uses it would be much wiser for us to go for them to a man who is merely holding land in order to compel those who would improve it to pay him a high price.

"Whether I am a fool or a philosopher, a philanthropist or an incendiary, there is one thing I am firmly convinced of — that houses and factories and steamships and railroads, and dry goods and groceries are good things for any community to have, and that that is the richest community that has most of them.

"Now, the more you tax those things the less of them you will have; but tax the value of land as much as you please and you will have none the less land, and it will be none the less useful. Tax land up to its full value and what would happen? Why simply that those who are holding land of which they make no use, would be compelled to give it up, and that those who wanted to make use of it could go and take it and improve it and use it without paying to the non-user anything for the privilege.

"Consider, gentlemen, how this city would grow, how enormously wealth would increase, if all taxes were abolished which now bear on the production and accumulation and exchange of wealth. Consider how quickly the vacant spaces on this island would fill up could land not improved, be had by them who wanted to improve it, without the payment of the prices now demanded. Then extend your view to the whole country and see how the same policy would everywhere enormously increase wealth."

In this frank exposition of his theories of home reform, their suggestor overlooks some points important to their value. His "old Dutchman" for example, is typical for the descendant of the first white settler from Holland on the island of "Outre Mer" and as such has at least the same rights as though he had been descended from the early natives of any Isle however fair and green, has long since ceased to own any considerable part of it. The territory is already largely covered besides his "old boots and glass bottles" with the shanties of what is known as a squatter colonization who usually pay no rent and often reluctantly yield to dispossession before the progress of a more permanent improvement.

On the other hand the poor old Dutchman has submitted for years to the exactions of repeated assessments, valuable to the contractor and the politician, as a means of subsistence to a constituency, in which the owner as a unit is disregarded where the greatest good is sought for the greatest number. Moreover he overlooks what the records will show, that a large portion of this property has already been sold for taxes, and assessments too onerous to be paid on wholly unproductive property, and that his additional taxes would be only a further lien on what is already forfeited or mainly for sale at far less than its accumulated cost. That to raise the enormous expenses of the city, unprecedented in the world for its area, would be like the nourishment of the Pelican which is said to feed on its own blood, or gleaning a field after it had been both harvested and pastured upon. The tax bills alone would soon cover its area as with a blanket.

His friend should realize before any location, what those longer familiar with the subject have learned; to count in the cost the yearly reminder of this past civic extravagance, and its present increase in his estimate of its use, or else to put on green goggles, and affect to be nourished by that dish of shavings, however annually cooked and set before him. In many cases he can "for further information apply on the premises" for corroboration of these suggestions.

He also neglects to tell, where, when all of this territory is improved by the result of industry, the next field for the imposition of new taxes which with death alone are certain, is to be found. Would not knowledge of such material points in the political economy of his own country, give value to suggestions as to the internal difficulties of any other. In seeking for any undiscovered field for additional taxation, on the island of "Outre Mer," he might aid the assessors, and also answer Mr. Pitt's pungent query, "Gentle Shepherd, tell me where ? "

APPENDIX E.

REPUTATION AT THE CANNON'S MOUTH AND THE CHANCES IN ITS TRANSMISSION (note, page 24).

Dr. Timothy Dwight, as the nephew of General Lyman, who with his father was an early settler of the Territory of the Natchez, at least showed a natural sentiment in vindicating the claim of his uncle as a worthy subordinate, to the merit he considered his due. Errors have always been claimed to exist in the distribution of credit for service. Time long since accorded the glory of two important victories to Sir William Johnson—one at Lake George in the summer of 1755, when Baron Dieskau, a veteran of the Continental Wars was defeated, another the capture of Niagara, four years later. The whole life of that self-educated soldier, had in all its details been sustained by his gallantry, and he early carried his son to the field to teach him the art of war. Possibly he may have been remiss as Dr. Dwight has claimed, in distributing some of his laurels to his officers, or the New England troops disposed, in the existing jealousy, to claim too many of them. The moment of victory has proved best adapted to settle relative merit, while all present are familiar with facts from observation. That passed, it has often proved as difficult where the credit of victory naturally falls to the Commander—as to ascertain now who aided to win the laurels of Caesar, Hannibal or Philip, if without record in history.

In cases of disaster, the blame at once falls upon the leader, regardless of who stumbled, and no one competes for a share. His son and successor probably fought as bravely in his detested invasions, and yet wears in some history the willow decreed to failure. Many of the friends of General de Peyster, will be gratified in his probable success in vindicating the honor and courage of his relative.

Mrs. Grundy in her "Observations in Utopia" refers to a notable case of another military muddle in its history, she says :

"There was some difference of opinion here, some time since, as to the advantage of the correction of accepted historical error, too late for practical use. In its course, a case was cited as occurring in the former wars of Utopia. It was occasioned by the carelessness or paramount personal engagements of a civilian acting as Secretary to a former honored Commander-in-Chief, Marshal Dauntless, an approved soldier."

"That gallant officer, had intended to lead the attack in person, at the great battle of "Ouvrir la Porte," and to head his forces, as he had often done. He had prepared the plan of the engagement before it occurred, showing his special command in the advance. The burning of a bridge in front of his position, preventing his reaching that post in season, caused him to alter his plan on the day before the attack and to order General Fearless, his second in command to advance with his light division, giving him an opportunity substantially to flank the fortifications, necessarily passing under a heavy fire and to attack the enemy supporting them in great force, if he found it practicable, before he — with every possible exertion — could come to his relief with the needed support of heavier artillery, and equalize the struggle, and shell out the batteries. The division commander with a very inadequate force, and mainly with a small section of it, only succeeded by a desperate *coup de main* in passing the works, meeting at and above them, the entire force of the enemy and mainly fighting the battle with the single division in the advance, before his commander could possibly reach the enemy and gallantly complete the victory, Gen. Fearless reaching the important post above them in advance of all support, and when the Marshal came up, landed, and received its surrender."

"After that great triumph, the commander of the entire force, to whom the honor of both its conception and achievement would naturally be given, sent his division commander — whom he loved, with the intelligence, to the seat of government, intending that he should receive his reward in thanks and promotion for the glory he had so materially aided in securing eventually for himself, as Napoleon alone concentrated in due season the glory of the Egyptian campaign, and Nelson that of the Nile."

"But alas! the Citizen Secretary had affixed to the report, which was not particular in detail, the old diagram of the proposed battle instead of that of the one *that was actually fought* which had been duly prepared, so falsifying his explanations. The division commander's statements were discredited by the papers he carried; history of this notable feat of arms was written and illustrations executed at once, based on the erroneous account, in most of which the real leader was not referred to or included, as all present knew to be due. All this mortification fell upon the gallant division commander, in place of the merit his remarkable achievement claimed, and although the Commander-in-Chief made ample correction of the records, and of the blunder of his subordinate, some years after when convinced of his error, the wound the mistake had given to a sensitive and modest nature, went with him to the grave. The Secretary yet survives, but some of the people here think he was a little more careless as to the record of another than he could have been of his own, and wonder that when he read the accounts, every where printed, of his conjectured position in the line on that old battle day, he too did not do something for *history*, by correcting *his* contribution to *its* many errors." To avoid such delay, and to correct an error yet palpable; it is proper to say after closer research, that Sir William offered the succession to the Superintendency of Indian Affairs, to his son in his lifetime, and that he asked to be relieved from its duties (page 51).

It is claimed that Lieut. Governor Colden—whose valuable "History of the Five Nations" had been published in 1727, and shows his knowledge of this trust—urged its acceptance on Sir John. His power to confer it, was through the absence of Governor Tryon, as Col. Guy's letter predicted. Another clerical error, occurs on page 71, stating that Col. Bouquet was born *at* and not *in* Switzerland, and one on page 74, places Colonel Lee, where Colonel William Washington actually was, waiting for equipments soon effectually used at Cowpens.

As to the Indian schools (page 66), new light has shown that this wise humanity is due more to personal benevolence than to the liberality of the Government.

It has been sometimes asked, why such historical papers as the handful used in the preceding pamphlet, *are not in the public archives*. The answer might be made that few things are in their proper place and yet many are useful.

The fact came to the writer from Mr. Francis A. Stout, a Commissioner of the State Survey, that by the defect of earlier Cartography, many places are found located *even miles* away from their actual geometrical position. And yet generations have lived and died in them, and there is probably no diminution of the area or acreage, which some would realize more than this defective location.

When visiting our State Capital some years since—in connection with his project of International Exchange—M. Alexandre Vattemare, found men in one of its chambers packing in boxes the recently printed "Documentary History," knee deep in old manuscripts, which *were* history, but used as fillers.

On his thoughtful suggestion to the Legislature, that these were not being *correctly located*, action was taken for the conservation of what remained; and the learned Dr. E. B. O'Callaghan—to whom we owe so much of our State History and from whom the writer had this fact, was created Curator, and laboriously catalogued those relics. Even afterwards—certainly without his knowledge, some were abstracted and Mr. John Bigelow, when Secretary of State, properly sought to reclaim them; even by circulars addressed to private collectors.

Curious papers often pass through many hands, as a merchantable article, and their migrations are also as indefinite as those of a circulating bill. Three of the grand collections of Historical manuscripts, once belonging to Rev. Dr. Sprague, of Albany, Mr. Robert Gilmor, of Baltimore, and Mr. Tefft of Savanah, have been broken up, the former, after it had been offered to the Government and State unsuccessfully, fell into the already large collection, of a private gentleman in Philadelphia, where it is likely to be preserved.

During the Civil War; as one of its evils, the high price of old paper, while the cruisers ruled commerce and shut out other material, brought out from many garrets and similar receptacles, a store of historical material of forgotten, or unknown value, to feed the paper mills, and weave material for the transmission of later facts. It is believed that more unprinted history, was then ground up, than even now exist in public or private collections.

It is stated that at that time, many old papers were discovered and exhumed from the outbuildings of Johnson Hall, possibly some containing the key to *this* research. Such papers are rarely sought for public collections when exposed at public or private sale, but fall, on conditions showing at least consideration for the value of the lives of others—into the private collections of a few antiquarians, sometimes to be reduced to print for private circulation.

Many find their way from Europe, especially from England. Lately the military papers of Lord Rawdon and Sir Henry Clinton, including beautifully executed military maps made by the Royal Engineers in America have been broken up and distributed here.

As an illustration of devotion to such collection and its accomplishments, it is only just to say, that there does not probably exist a more comprehensive memorial of the men of mark who have been connected with American History since the settlements, than that formed by Dr. Emmett—elsewhere referred to. That hidden in his library and known only to few, in notably fine condition, by restoration and exhaustive illustration with portraits and views, is probably the most valuable and intelligible monument to them, erected by a single hand, from many sources, in hours devoted to recreation in an active and useful life. There are a number of others, very complete and interesting, even superior to it in some details, but as an entirety it may claim to be unequalled in condition, and it is the result of years of research.

An incident which has occurred before this Appendix is printed, is referred to as practically sustaining some of the views which have been suggested. How supply and demand govern value, how it is increased when a thing is put in the right place, and how recognition of the past shows solid progress in the present.

The venerable Robert C. Winthrop, has done a good work, in restoring the portrait of one by whom his life has been doubtless influenced; additionally so as the friendly act of a representative of early patriotism in Massachusetts, in sympathizing with those of South Carolina. The old City Hall, of Charleston, South Carolina, had been completely restored and beautified, the interior entirely rebuilt with twelve spacious rooms, all with a remarkable economy ($20,000), creditable to the city officials, and suggestive to those of other cities.

In its park, a life sized statue of Pitt, Earl of Chatham, erected by the citizens in their gratitude for the repeal of the Stamp Act, and thrown down after Clinton's capture, has been remounted on a new pedestal, with the old inscription tablet sought out and replaced. Even the signs of mutilation are suggestive to patriotism and of a possible similar restoration of its headless *replique*, in the keeping of the New York Historical Society.

The Common Council and citizens of Charleston, showing their appreciation of the renewal of their civic home, assembled on the 15th of November, for its rededication. The Mayor — Mr. Courtenay, whose heart had been in this work, made a suggestive opening address, effectively recalling the early history of the city, its position, and his hopes in its course, referring to the services of his first predecessor — after the Intendancy — the distinguished Robert Y. Hayne; who had accepted the position, after serving as Governor and United States Senator. He showed how Hayne had labored for facilities of communication with the interior, and for the progress of the city, incidentally comparing these details of his life to those of De Witt Clinton. He then recalled a resolution passed by the citizens on his decease in 1839, to place his marble bust in the City Hall, and suggested its re-enactment, which, after other spirited addresses, was unanimously adopted. As the News and Courier reports :

"Mayor Courtenay then said : During the visit of Governor Winthrop to this city in 1880, he visited the Council Chamber to see the portraits and other works of art owned by. the city. He called the attention to the neglected condition of "Trumbull's Washington," a full length portrait of great value and historic interest, and urged that it be placed in proper hands for restoration, proffering his services in advising and superintending the work. By unanimous vote of the City Council the picture was forwarded to Governor Winthrop, and has been wonderfully renewed, and now presents as fine an appearance as when originally painted. It was completed last spring, and was received in the Boston Museum of Art and kept on exhibition during the summer and fall months, and is again restored to its familiar place on the walls of our chamber. Alderman Rogers thereupon offered the following resolution : WHEREAS, Our distinguished fellow countryman, Governor Winthrop, of Massachusetts, while on a visit to this city in 1880, and enjoying its relics of our olden time, became greatly interested in the preservation of our Trumbull's Washington, and wisely suggested its repair and restoration, and to further this end offered his most valuable services of supervision and care of this work; and whereas, through his kind offices the work of restoration has now been finally completed, and this valued picture of our city, now in its old power and life, again adorns our walls. Be it, therefore, *Resolved*, That the City Council of Charleston gratefully acknowledge and appreciate the valuable aid and kind personal service of Governor Winthrop in the successful accomplishment of the work of restoration of our great painting of Trumbull's Washington. The resolution was unanimously adopted.

The Mayor announced to Council that Mr. T. Bailey Myers, of New York city, had presented to the city three rare and valuable engravings of great local interest to our citizens: 1. Sir Henry Clinton's map of the siege of Charleston, 1780, showing the city and the harbor, surrounding country, the fortifications, and position of the fleet under Vice-Admiral Mariot Arbuthnot. 2. An engraved portrait of William Pitt, Earl of Chatham, Secretary of State from the year 1757 to 1768, by James Barry, R. A., September, 1778. 3. "An exact prospect of Charleston, the metropolis of the Province of South Carolina, an original engraving published in the *London Magazine*, June, 1762." In this connection, Alderman White — after a preamble again describing this small contribution, which is *here* omitted — "presented the following resolutions: Be it *Resolved*, That the thanks of the City Council are due and hereby tendered to Mr. T. Bailey Myers for these valued gifts, and we assure him that his liberality is highly appreciated by the citizens of Charleston. *Resolved*, That these engravings be hung on the walls of the mayor's office and carefully preserved as objects of general interest to our community. These resolutions were also unanimously adopted." Such recollection of past traditions, in an ancient city, which gallantly resisted royalist, loyalist and tory, in the period to which these things refer, is a pleasant evidence of adhesion to early sympathies, and to the united action of the infant states.

Since the foregoing paper has been printed, even its delay for some illustration, has evidenced how the rapid progress of the world affects the smallest atom. Its suggestion of the claim of "History as a Fine Art," has been by a gratifying coincidence, in that interval sustained — with his usual ability — by the Rev. Dr. Howard Crosby, in a paper presented before the Seventy-eighth Anniversary Meeting of the New York Historical Society, while the changes in the method of correspondence, has also lately recalled editorial notice in the columns of the "Times.'

Concurrence of thought, we know naturally exists as to many subjects of varied importance in a nation of fifty millions, including great intelligence. Differences of conclusion are often more conspicuous. The comparison of opinions in public in any form, may demonstrate the value of convictions to some, call forth the sympathy of others, who have entertained without expressing them, or at least open them to correction. Thought has always been considered a safe predecessor to action.

At least, in public affairs it would appear that advanced methods of legislation claim careful deliberate consideration by their presentors as well as by the representative, and that hasty action is only justified where circumstances demand the experiment. This admitted, Dr. Crosby, who as a private citizen takes an active interest in current public administration, might be induced hereafter to show, how the entire record of American statesmanship — conformed to the example of many of its former and present elements, was affording a noble example of self devotion in constructing history, and that the creation as well as the condensation, had just claim to be considered as a fine Art.

Many wise and pertinent suggestions, contained in the President's recent message, appear to offer material for the action of statesmanship, rising above party or local considerations, and according with a widely expressed sentiment in favor of such more considerate and prudent legislation as would seem to best assure the prosperity and permanency of our institutions.

www.ingramcontent.com/pod-product-compliance
Lightning Source LLC
Chambersburg PA
CBHW020121170426
43199CB00009B/582